Integrated
Management Systems

Also available from ASQ Quality Press

Principles of Quality Costs: Financial Measures for Strategic Implementation of Quality Management, Fourth Edition
Douglas C. Wood, editor

Making Change Work: Practical Tools for Overcoming Human Resistance to Change
Brien Palmer

Office Kaizen: Transforming Office Operations into a Strategic Competitive Advantage
William Lareau

The Quality Toolbox, Second Edition
Nancy R. Tague

Root Cause Analysis: Simplified Tools and Techniques, Second Edition
Bjørn Andersen and Tom Fagerhaug

The Certified Six Sigma Green Belt Handbook, Second Edition
Roderick A. Munro, Govindarajan Ramu, and Daniel J. Zrymiak

The Certified Manager of Quality/Organizational Excellence Handbook, Fourth Edition
Russell T. Westcott, editor

The Certified Six Sigma Black Belt Handbook, Second Edition
T.M. Kubiak and Donald W. Benbow

The ASQ Auditing Handbook, Fourth Edition
J.P. Russell, editor

The ASQ Quality Improvement Pocket Guide: Basic History, Concepts, Tools, and Relationships
Grace L. Duffy, editor

Process Driven Comprehensive Auditing: A New Way to Conduct ISO 9001:2008 Internal Audits, Second Edition
Paul C. Palmes

Using ISO 9001 in Healthcare: Applications for Quality Systems, Performance Improvement, Clinical Integration, and Accreditation
James M. Levett, MD and Robert G. Burney, MD

To request a complimentary catalog of ASQ Quality Press publications, call 800-248-1946, or visit our Web site at http://www.asq.org/quality-press.

Integrated Management Systems

QMS, EMS, OHSMS, FSMS including
Aerospace, Service, Semiconductor /
Electronics, Automotive, and Food

*Updated to the latest standard changes including
ISO 9001:2015, ISO 14001:2015, and ISO 45001:2016*

*Includes guidance on integrating
Corporate Responsibility and Sustainability*

Chad Kymal, Gregory Gruska, and R. Dan Reid

ASQ Quality Press
Milwaukee, Wisconsin

American Society for Quality, Quality Press, Milwaukee, WI 53203
© 2015 by ASQ.
All rights reserved. Published 2015.
Printed in the United States of America.

20 19 18 17 16 15   5 4 3 2 1

Library of Congress Cataloging-in-Publication Data

Kymal, Chad.
Integrated management systems: QMS, EMS, OHSMS, FSMS including aerospace,
service, semiconductor/elecrtronics, automotive, and food / by Chad Kymal,
Gregory Gruska, and R. Dan Reid.
    pages cm
ISBN 978-0-87389-894-2 (hardcover: alk. paper)
1. Quality control—Management. 2. Quality control—Standards. 3. Management
information systems. I. Gruska, Gregory F., 1943- II. Reid, R. Dan (Robert Dan), 1949-
III. Title.
TS156.K96 2014
658.5'620218—dc23
                        2014040874

Publisher: Lynelle Korte
Acquisitions Editor: Matt T. Meinholz
Managing Editor: Paul Daniel O'Mara
Production Administrator: Randall Benson

ASQ Mission: The American Society for Quality advances individual, organizational,
and community excellence worldwide through learning, quality improvement, and
knowledge exchange.

Attention Bookstores, Wholesalers, Schools, and Corporations: ASQ Quality Press books,
video, audio, and software are available at quantity discounts with bulk purchases for
business, educational, or instructional use. For information, please contact ASQ Quality
Press at 800-248-1946, or write to ASQ Quality Press, P.O. Box 3005, Milwaukee, WI
53201-3005.

To place orders or to request ASQ membership information, call 800-248-1946. Visit our
Web site at www.asq.org/quality-press.

∞ Printed on acid-free paper

Quality Press
600 N. Plankinton Ave.
Milwaukee, WI 53203-2914
E-mail: authors@asq.org

ASQ   **The Global Voice of Quality**™

Contents

Chapters

Figures and Tables

Preface

Organizations today are implementing stand-alone systems for their Quality Management Systems (ISO 9001, ISO/TS 16949, or AS9100), Environmental Management System (ISO 14001), Occupational Health & Safety (ISO 45001), and Food Safety Management Systems (FSSC 22000). Stand-alone systems refer to the use of isolated document management structures resulting in the duplication of processes within one site for each of the management standards—QMS, EMS, OHSMS, and FSMS. In other words, the stand-alone systems duplicate training processes, document control, and internal audit processes for each standard within the company. While the confusion and lack of efficiency resulting from this decision may not be readily apparent to the uninitiated, this book will show the reader that there is a tremendous loss of value associated with stand-alone management systems within an organization.

Worse yet, many organizations continue this duplication of effort among their different sites—including plants, design centers, and sales offices. If there is a lack of efficiency and confusion caused by the duplication in one site, one can imagine the magnification of these same problems when duplication is repeated multiple times in a large organization. The paper "Juggling multiple standards," published by this author in 2005, provided a case study of a large European organization and included examples of duplication of management reviews and risk assessments. This same organization had processes such as document control that were repeated no less than 30 to 50 times in their large sites (called campuses) in Silicon Valley or in France.

The reduction of process duplication within one organization is referred to as *integration* and the reduction of duplication between sites is referred to as *standardization*. Figure 0.1 illustrates a situation in which the organization is implementing ISO/TS 16949, ISO 14001, and ISO 45001. This graphic is easily extended, as the organization intends to implement other standards such as FSSC 22000, ISO 26000, and so on. This book addresses both lack of integration and lack of standardization. It is a rare occasion when one can read about both topics in one paper or book, although the importance of both integration and standardization to the efficiency of implementation and maintenance of a management system cannot be overstated.

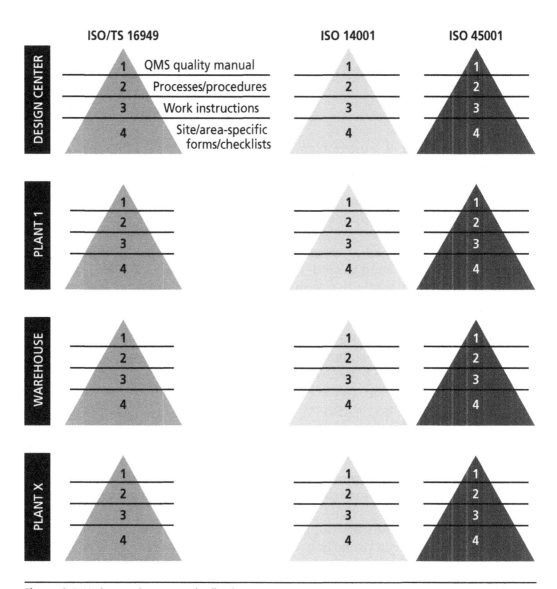

Figure 0.1 No integration or standardization.

Note: *Integration* refers to the processes within one site (horizontal in this illustration), while *standardization* refers to processes between sites (vertical in this illustration).

The time for integration and standardization has arrived as organizations are beginning to realize that applying these concepts effectively will produce significant savings. The authors estimate that integration reduces implementation costs by 50% and maintenance costs by 66%. Also, third-party auditing costs are reduced by more than 20%.

Integration and standardization can be applied to service and manufacturing organizations in industries such as automotive, aerospace, and food services. This book will cover the key principles of integrated management systems and includes case studies of its application in a variety of industries.

Integrating and standardizing processes companywide is an important task of quality professionals globally. It is vital to how business processes are managed, including the measurement and monitoring of their effectiveness, and it has far reaching implications on how an organization operates globally. We hope this book provides a guide and road map for organizations wanting to achieve integration and standardization. Omnex's 30 years of experience in this subject will be put to good use in this book and its companion books on auditing and implementation.

The first article written by this author was on standardization of management systems in 1995 as Omnex implemented standardized processes for 27 Kelsey Hayes plants (now ZF). The first integration article, "Juggling Multiple Standards—Save time and money by integrating your various management systems," was written in 2005. This article reflected the experience we had gained in the first integration project, where we integrated and standardized processes between the QMS and EMS for Yazaki of North America in 2001. Also, while Chad Kymal was the Chairman of the international registrar AQSR (headquartered in Ann Arbor), we prided ourselves in having 14 lead auditors who could conduct integrated audits to QMS, EMS, and OHSMS.

Implementing integrated management systems starts with top management. They need to understand the inherent value to a global organization. The more spread out the organization, the more it needs both standardization and integration of processes. Customers frequently tell large multinational organizations that they want their plants in the United States, India, and China to work in the "same way" with the customer. How can this be possible? The answer is, of course, standardized and integrated enterprise processes company wide. While a strong company culture is important, it is the processes that make an organization what it is.

We have much to say about designing efficient and effective enterprise processes. The authors have spoken and written about it in many presentations and papers. However, this book will not be the venue for this important topic. It will have to wait for another suitable book. However, top management needs to adopt and enforce common and integrated processes globally, with no "ifs, ands, or buts." Top management should show little leeway or tolerance for reasons why plants or regions cannot standardize.

ISO 9001 and ISO 14001 are changing in 2015 and ISO 45001, the revised OHSAS 18001 which is being introduced in 2016. In a matter of two years all three standards are changing. Along with the change, the standards are adopting a common structure or format. This high level structure commonly adopted by all three standards is good for integration. The change in the standards and the high level structure should really spur integration and standardization globally.

This book introduces integrated management systems (IMS) in Chapter 1. Generally speaking, integrated management systems satisfy all applicable management systems including quality, environmental, health and safety, and food safety (QMS, EMS, OHSMS, and FSMS). The authors define integrated management systems in one site as integrated processes, integrated risk, and integrated audits. Fundamental ideas and definitions of IMS will be introduced in Chapter 1.

In Chapter 2 the IMS in one site will be extended to the enterprise with the ideas of integration and standardization for processes, risks, and audits. Fundamental ideas of enterprise integration and standardization, along with definitions and cost savings, will be presented in Chapter 2.

In Chapters 3, 4, and 5 the book will explain integration and standardization in detail, single site and enterprise implementations for processes, risk, and audits. Chapter 6 will describe the Best in Class implementations of IMS, which will be expanded upon in the third book in this series on integrated management systems.

Chapters 7, 8, 9, 10, and 11 will describe implementations Omnex conducted globally in Asia, the Middle East, and USA/Europe in the aerospace, service, semiconductor/electronics, automotive, and food management systems. Chapter 12 will describe an important class of software called EwIMS. It is our opinion that it is close to impossible to implement integrated management systems without it. Chapter 13 will take a critical look at the pros and cons in each implementation and describe lessons learned from implementing IMS at a site or an enterprise. Chapter 14 will describe how the authors integrate the clauses and requirements and the methodology and process needed.

We hope this book contributes to the understanding of integrated management systems globally. There is much to learn and understand about enterprise IMS. It not only saves money, but more importantly it contributes to the maintenance and efficiency of business processes and conformance standards such as ISO 9001, AS9100, ISO/TS 16949, ISO 14001, ISO 45001, and FSSC 22000 or other GFSI Standards.

There are three books planned in this series, including *Integrated Management Systems Implementation, Integrated Management Systems Auditing and Designing* and *Implementing Best In Class Processes in an Integrated Management System.*

About the Authors

CHAD KYMAL

Chad Kymal is the CTO and founder of Omnex Inc., an international consulting and training organization headquartered in the United States. After graduating from the General Motors Institute, Chad spent a number of years working at General Motors and KPMG before founding Omnex Inc. in 1986. Over the course of Chad's successful career, he has served on the Malcolm Baldrige Board of Examiners and has received numerous quality achievement awards, including the Quality Professional of the Year award by the American Society for Quality (ASQ) Automotive Division in 2005. In addition to his bachelor's degree from GMI, Chad holds both a master's degree in industrial and operations engineering from the University of Michigan and an MBA from the University of Michigan.

Chad both developed and teaches auditor training for ISO 9001, ISO 14001, and OHSAS 18001/ISO 45001, as well as an Integrated Management Systems Lead Auditor training course where all three standards are combined in a single audit. Chad is the founder of AQSR, a global registrar that routinely provided integrated audits in QMS, EMS, and OHSMS.

Chad is the author of four books and more than 100 papers including several on integrated management systems.

R. DAN REID

R. Dan Reid, the Omnex Director of Consulting, is best known as an author of *QS-9000, ISO Technical Specification (TS) 16949, ISO 9001:2000,* the first ISO International Workshop Agreement (IWA 1), which applies ISO 9001 to healthcare and its replacement, AIAG's Business Operating Systems for Healthcare Organizations (HF-2). He also worked on the Chrysler, Ford, and GM *Potential Failure Mode and Effects Analysis, Production Part Approval Process, and Advanced Product Quality Planning* manuals.

While at AIAG, Dan led successful projects for Effective Problem Solving, Cost of Poor Quality, and Supplier Management. While at General Motors, among other assignments, he led the Supplier Development Administration, served on the Chrysler, Ford, GM Supplier Quality Requirements Task Force, which was responsible for QS-9000 and later ISO/TS 16949, and he established a Supplier Quality function at GM Service Parts. He later established a Supplier Quality function at Baxter BioScience Division's Los Angeles plant before serving as the BioScience Divisional Supplier Quality Director.

Dan, an ASQ Fellow and ASQ Certified Quality Engineer (CQE), has received numerous awards and is recognized for a number of accomplishments:

- The first Delegation Leader of the International Automotive Task Force (IATF)
- A member of the Parenteral Drug Association
- A member of the American College of Health Care Executives
- A published author with McGraw Hill, ASQ Quality Press, and others
- A member of the ASQ Administrative Committee and Technical Reviewer
- On the A2LA Board of Directors

GREG GRUSKA

Greg Gruska, a Fellow of ASQ, is the principal consultant in performance excellence for Omnex. Greg is a member of the team that developed the new AIAG Effective Problem Solving guideline for practitioners and leaders (CQI-20 and CQI-21). He has taught and assisted hundreds of practitioners in problem solving methodologies and tools.

Greg is also an active/writing member of the MSA, SPC, FMEA, EFMEA, and EPS Manual subcommittees of the American Automotive Industry Group (AIAG) Supplier Quality Requirements Task Force, which is part of the international task force governing ISO/TS 16949. Greg is an adjunct professor at Madonna University. He has advanced degrees in mathematics and engineering from the University of Detroit, Michigan State University, and Wayne State University. He was the Deming Memorial Lecturer at the Sheffield Hallam University for the year 2000.

Greg is a charter member of the Greater Detroit Deming Study Group and the W. E. Deming Institute. He is an ASQ-certified Quality Engineer, a licensed Professional Engineer (CA – Quality), and a member of the Board of Examiners of and Judge for the Michigan Quality Leadership Award (1994-2011). Greg is on the writing committee of AIAG on FMEA, a member of the SAE Functional Safety Committee (J2980), and considered one of the foremost authorities on risk management in the world. He has considerable hardware and software experience in automotive applications.

1

What are Integrated Management Systems, including PAS 99?

INTRODUCTION

L et us start with an example. One of our customers has 80 plants around the world. They have implemented a QMS (Quality Management Systems, ISO 9001 or another version of it), an EMS (Environmental Management Systems, ISO 14001), and an LBMS (Laboratory Management Systems, ISO 17025) in the US plants and in European and Asian plants. In addition, they have implemented OHSMS (Health and Safety Management Systems, ISO 45001) in the European and Asian plants. This customer is not standardized or integrated. Although every one of their 80 plants follows corporate guidelines, each developed and uses unique sets of policies and procedures for the various standards.

Unfortunately, our client is not unique. Organizations today are implementing individual stand-alone systems to achieve different business strategies; for example, for their QMS (ISO 9001, ISO/TS 16949, or AS9100), EMS (ISO 14001), and OHSMS (ISO 45001). Worse yet, each of their sites—plants, design centers, and sales offices—is developing its own systems to achieve the same results. At best, this lack of consistency will result in a loss of efficiency and effectiveness; at worst, it can create chaotic situations within the organization.

The reduction of duplication of similar processes within one organization between management standards is referred to as *integration*; the reduction of duplication of similar processes between sites is referred to as *standardization*. See Figure 1.1.

We request that the reader be patient in understanding the fundamentals of integration in one site in Chapter 1 and then enterprise integration that is introduced in Chapter 2. There is much new information to be covered in the next few chapters.

INTEGRATED PROCESSES

To understand how to achieve integration and standardization, let us start with an organization with a single site.

So what does integration mean in the context of a single site? The extent of integration or non-integration is indicated by the answers to the following questions:

- Are the manuals or level I documents in the QMS, EMS, or OHSMS integrated or non-integrated?

- Are the procedures or level II documents in the QMS, EMS, or OHSMS integrated or non-integrated? What percentage of the procedures are the same between the standards you are considering?

- Are the work instructions or level III documents in the QMS, EMS, or OHSMS integrated or non-integrated? What percentage of the procedures are the same between the standards you are considering?

- Are the forms and checklists or level IV documents in the QMS, EMS, or OHSMS integrated or non-integrated? What percentage of the procedures are the same between the standards you are considering?

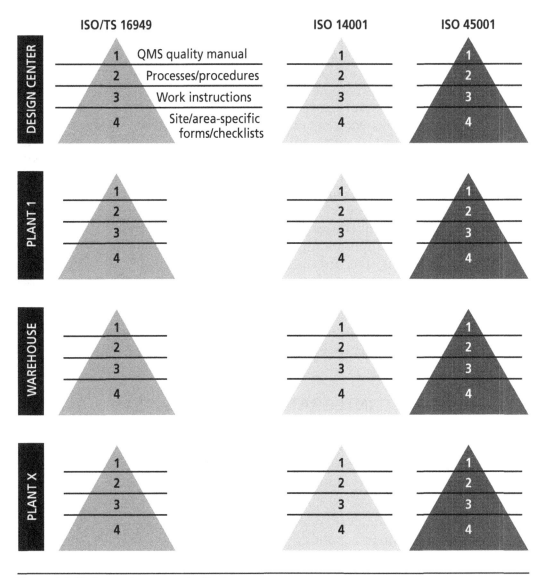

Figure 1.1 No integration or standardization.

Management systems are considered integrated if they have 70% to 95% integration for the procedures and at least 30% for work instructions. For a process or work instruction to be fully integrated, it is not enough for it to be one documented process; it should be managed by one process owner in order for the organization to get the full benefits of integration. For example, if the training procedure is identical for the QMS and EMS, it is integrated, but if it is managed by two different process owners, then the company gets savings during implementation of the management system, but not enough in its maintenance. The matrix below, Table 1.1, shows in tabular form what is integrated and what is not.

Let us assume that there are only four processes in this organization. If we did, we would reach the following conclusions: QMS, EMS, and OHSMS are 33% integrated. The process ownership is 0% since there is no common process owner. Overall, then, in one site that has three standards, the overall process integration and process ownership integration number is the smaller number when each standard is compared to the others. In other words, one process out of three is integrated between the three standards and none of the process owners are common between the processes.

Completing this matrix requires understanding that document control, records control, and policy, objectives, and planning can be integrated in the QMS, EMS, and OHSMS management systems. We will provide tables in later chapters so that organizations can analyze their own integration numbers.

Should all processes be integrated? The answer is no. Organizations need to determine what they want and do not want to integrate. For example, a large organization may decide that it wants business plan objectives, QMS objectives, EMS objectives, and OHSMS objectives to be set by different groups. Of course, we believe that one process would have sufficed and we think integration is the

Table 1.1 Process integration matrix (single site).

QMS			EMS				OHSMS			
Process Name	Procedure Number	Process Owner	Process Name	Procedure Number	Process Owner	INT	Process Name	Procedure Number	Process Owner	INT
Document Control	SOP-12	John Black	Same		Meg Ryan	Y	Document Control	OH-22	Kevin Rogers	Y
Records Control	SOP-14	Jim Johnson	Same		Jim Johnson	Y	Records Control	OH-15	Kevin Rogers	N
Policy, Objectives, and Business Planning	SOP-22	Kathy Down	Policy, EMS Planning	EMS-5		N	Policy and OH Planning	OH-17	Kevin Rogers	N
Integration			66% (2/3)		33% (1/3)	66% (2/3)	0%		0	33%

best practice; however, sometimes integration runs into organizational turf wars. To accommodate organizational and business-related structural issues, we offer the range of 70% to 95% as a good target for global organizations for process integration and process ownership integration.

This is the first time the integration of one site and the process owner assignment has been quantified in an integrated management system. However, as seen in the example in Table 1.1, we are not finished; this study has to be conducted for each of the organization's sites, including design. The standardization of processes across the enterprise is the next number that can be quantified. We will do this in the next chapter on enterprise standardization.

Integrated Processes

Standalone systems are systems that score between 0 and 70% when analyzed using an integration matrix for either the process or process owner integration.

Integrated management systems are defined as management systems (processes) that score 70% to 95% for both process and process owner integration using an integration matrix.

Integrated processes are usually what is referred to when organizations discuss integrated management systems. In fact, there are three key aspects to integration—processes, risk, and audits. Each of these must be integrated (and standardized in an enterprise) for additional organizational efficiency. See Figure 1.2.

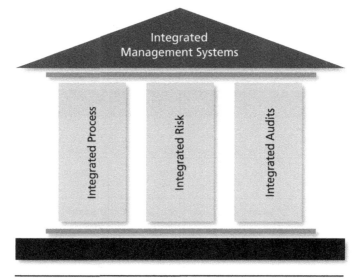

Figure 1.2 Three pillars of an integrated management system.

INTEGRATED RISK

To be successful, organizations need to understand the various risks that can affect their business. Specifically, organizations need to evaluate quality, environmental, and health and safety risks. QMS, EMS, and OHSMS require risk evaluation within the organization with controls in place for the highest risk items. The new ISO 9001, released in 2015, will require risk evaluation for quality within the organization. Standards such as AS9100 (aerospace), ISO/TS 16949 (automotive), and ISO 13485 (medical devices) all require risk evaluation in the product realization processes. Food Safety Management Systems (FSMS) compliant to GFSI standards require risk assessment for food safety. SQF, a version of the GFSI standard, has both food safety and quality incorporated within the standard for a level III certification. Integrating risk between QMS, EMS, OHSMS, and FSMS is the second level of integration for an IMS. So this is the second test for integration. This integration can be evaluated by asking the following questions:

- What is the risk management process used within the organization for QMS, EMS, OHSMS, FSMS, and other standards?
- Is a common system followed?
- Is there a standardization of the severity and occurrence ratings between the risk management process, so comparisons can be made between risk in the different categories of Q, E, HS, and FS? (Note: Risk = Sev x Occ.)

The risk methodology and risk ratings can be integrated and standardized within an organization. When integration takes place within a site, then the organization can understand and compare the risks between the categories of Q, E, HS, and FS (as applicable). If the risk methodology and risk ratings are standardized within the enterprise, then the risk can be compared within the entire enterprise. The organization can ask why the same process has a different rating in Q, E, or HS within two different sites. Or, if one site rates a risk high and another similar site has not included it at all, the organization can ask why not? Having an integrated and standardized system for risk evaluation, risk ratings, and risk management is a significant outcome of integrated management systems. In our opinion, this is the reason top management, customers, and shareholders are implementing standards such as QMS, EMS, OHSMS, and FSMS, that is, to reduce and manage risk. Top management today is sadly lacking in knowledge of the highest risks in their organizations for quality, environmental, health and safety, and food safety (as applicable).

In our example, there is 66% (2/3) risk integration; that is, two management systems out of the three are integrated (see Table 1.2).

Table 1.2 Integrated risk matrix example (single site).

QMS		EMS		OHSMS	
Risk Methodology	FMEA	Risk Methodology	FMEA	Risk Methodology (HAZOP)	Job Analysis
Risk Tables	Severity, Occurence, and Detection	Risk Tables	Integ	Risk Tables	No
Team	Cross Functional Process and Product Teams	Team	Same	Team	Health and Safety team
Integration			100%		0%

Definition of Integrated Risk in One Site

Integrated management systems have integrated risks (common risk methodology) between quality, environmental, health and safety, and food safety (Q, E, HS, and/or FS) and have comparable severity (Sev.) and occurrence (Occ.) risk ratings between the categories. Optimally, one team conducts the risk analysis for the three different categories.

INTEGRATED AUDITS

The next topic of discussion is integrated audits. This is the third element of an integrated management system. Integrated audits are inherently easy to understand and this is usually the first thought that occurs to most management system professionals when they think of integrated management systems. Of course, integrated audits can only be conducted when the processes within an organization are integrated. Here are the questions to ask to determine integrated audits for an integrated management system:

- Have the processes within an organization been integrated? (If the answer to this is no, then integrated audits cannot be conducted.)
- Has the auditing process been integrated within a site?
- Do integrated auditing process refer to the same audit calendar or schedule, audit process, integrated audit checklist?
- Is one conducted for Q, E, HS, and/or FS audit programs?

There are many more detailed questions to ask, but that can wait for the chapter on integrated audits.

Definition of Integrated Audits

The use of one common audit process and audit program for Q, E, HS, or FSMS management systems in one site. The audit process uses an integrated audit checklist and an audit team capable of auditing the integrated system.

In this example in Table 1.3, the same audit process, audit schedule, and team are used for QMS, EMS, and OHSMS resulting in a score of 100% for the site. However, integrated audits are only valid if the answer to the process integration question is a Yes. If not, then the score of the integrated audit is the same score of the integrated process or the lower of the two since integrated audits follow the axiom—you can only conduct an integrated audit for an integrated management system i.e. including integrated processes. Since the score for integrated processes is 33%, the integrated audit score is the smaller of the integrated audit and process integration score, which in this case is 33%.

Table 1.3 Integrated audit process example (single site).

	QMS	EMS	OHSMS	
Common Audit Program (includes schedule, audit schedule, and team)	SOP 22– Audit Process	Same Process	Same Process	Overall
Integrated		100%	100%	100%
Integrated Processes		NA	66%	33%

PAS 99

PAS 99 is a British Standards Institute standard published in 2006 and then revised in 2012. The PAS, or Publicly Available Standard, purports to be "primarily meant to be used by those organizations who are implementing the requirements of two or more Management Systems Standards (MSSs). The adoption of this PAS is intended to simplify the implementation of multiple system standards and any associated conformity assessment together with introducing some of the newer principles of management systems..." When commenting on the PAS 99:2006 standard, our remarks were "it is our opinion that the standard does not help companies understand or implement an integrated management standard. It discusses integration, but spends no time talking about standardization." The latest PAS published in 2012 is an improvement over the 2006 release. Although it is more useful, it still does not discuss standardization or the differences between site and enterprise implementations. The integration around the "Framework of Management System Standards" is a move in the right direction. The latest revision of the ISO 9001, ISO 14001, and ISO 45001 standards are being revised using a common High Level Structure (HLS), however this is still not useful enough.

The biggest plus point of this standard is that it has included common elements of all standards. However, there is not enough direction on developing integrated processes, risk, or audits. However, as the PAS 99 states in the Annex (guidance), "the PAS draws on the high level structure and common requirements provided… as a framework to implement two or more MSSs in an integrated way. In applying this high level framework for embracing the common requirements of MSSs and other management systems, it is important to recognize that there are specific requirements in individual specifications that are not included in the generic framework. Those requirements that are not common should be addressed in addition to those in PAS 99, in order to meet the specific standards and specifications to which the organization subscribes." Therein lies the weakness; common requirements are good, but those who are uninitiated will have a difficult time identifying the requirements that are not addressed by the PAS 99 (unique requirements not common) in the QMS, EMS, OHSMS, or other MSS standards.

The latest revision is a change in the right direction; it includes language about the process approach and including risk in the appendix. The ambiguity and generality in the instructions could probably reflect the diverse views of writing members and also the need for generality when addressing literally hundreds of management systems standards.

SUMMARY

This chapter provides the understanding and motivation for integrated management systems. Stated simply, integration refers to integrated processes, risks, and audits at one site. A definition of integrated processes, risks, audits, and matrices to provide a metric for integration are key breakthroughs of this chapter.

Table 1.4 illustrates the three matrices for integrated processes, risk, and audits for a single site. If there are only four processes in this organization, we would reach the conclusion that the QMS, EMS, and OHSMS are 33% integrated.

There is 66% (2/3) risk integration between the three management systems.

The audit process is integrated 100% between the EMS, QMS, and OHSMS. However, due to lack of integrated processes, the score will be reduced to 33% (the smaller of the two scores as discussed earlier). Simply said, though the audit score is 100%, the benefit to the organization is only 33% (since each of the processes that are not integrated need to be individually sampled).

Table 1.4 Single site process integration matrix.

QMS			EMS				OHSMS			
Process Name	Procedure Number	Process Owner	Process Name	Procedure Number	Process Owner	INT	Process Name	Procedure Number	Process Owner	INT
Document Control	SOP-12	John Black	Same		Meg Ryan	Y	Document Control	OH-22	Kevin Rogers	Y
Records Control	SOP-14	Jim Johnson	Same		Jim Johnson	Y	Records Control	OH-15	Kevin Rogers	N
Policy, Objectives, and Business Planning	SOP-22	Kathy Down	Policy, EMS Planning	EMS-5		N	Policy and OH Planning	OH-17	Kevin Rogers	N
Integration			66% (2/3)		33% (1/3)	66% (2/3)	0%		0	33%

QMS		EMS		OHSMS	
Risk Methodology	FMEA	Risk Methodology	FMEA	Risk Methodology	Job Analysis
Risk Tables	Severity, Occurence, and Detection	Risk Tables	Integ	Risk Tables	No
Team	Cross Functional Process and Product Teams	Team	Same	Team	Health and Safety team
Integrated			100%		0%

	QMS	EMS	OHSMS	
Common Audit Program (Includes schedule, audit schedule and team)	SOP 22 – Audit Process	Same Process	Same Process	Overall
Integrated		100%	100%	100%
Integrated Processes		NA	66%	33%

A summary of the integration in one site are illustrated here:

Site 1	
Process Integration	33%
Risk Integration	66%
Audit Integration	33%
Overall Single Site Integration Score	33 / 66 / 33

The 33/66/33 score refers to the scores for one site in the three different topics of integration—that is processes, risk, and audits. The best score would be 100/100/100. We could total the three scores (33 + 66 + 33) and divide by 3 to reach an average score of 44 (132/3 = 44).

The savings from integrated audits is 50% for implementation and 66% for maintenance. What this means is that the cost of implementation of three standards can be reduced by 50% and the ongoing maintenance costs can be reduced by 66% if the score was 100/100/100 and the management systems were fully integrated. In this case, the organization would save less than half of the projected savings (that is, 25% for implementation and 33% for maintenance). If the implementation costs were $200,000 for all three management systems and maintenance was $90,000/ year, then the company would be forgoing $50,000 of implementation costs (one time savings) and about $30,000 a year of maintenance costs.

There is one more savings, and that is savings from integrated third-party audits. We explained that integration saves 20% of external third-party audit costs. In this example, the organization would have to be more integrated before they could approach their registrar. If third-party auditing costs for QMS, EMS, and OHSMS are $45,000 for three years (30 days of external audits for three years including the recertification costs), then 20% would be $9000 every three years or $3,000 per year.

Following the guidelines of this chapter, organizations can begin to understand the characteristics of integration within one site of an organization. The next chapter provides insights on how to integrate within an enterprise, referred to as standardization—standardized processes, risk, and audits. There is much to be gained in terms of streamlined processes and savings with enterprise integration and standardization.

Savings from Integration for One Site

Assumptions: Cost of implementation of three management system standards, $200,000; maintenance costs, $90,000/year; and third-party auditing costs, $45,000 for three years.

Savings from implementation (one-time cost): $200,000 x .50 = $100,000.

Savings from maintenance: $90,000 x .66 = $60,000 per year at each site; NPV at 10% would be $600,000.

Maintenance includes maintaining stand-alone processes of QMS, EMS, and OHSMS, which will be combined to 1/3 of the previous total with 1/3 less process owners. Management reviews and internal audits will be 1.3 lower as well. Hence, maintenance of the QMS, EMS, and OHSMS will be reduced to 33% of the previous costs each year.

Savings from third-party audit costs: $1500 each year x .20; NPV is $30,000.

20% of the third-party audit costs: the reduction is provided by registrars for integrated audits. Up to 40% is allowed for organizations with more than 10 sites.

Total Savings: $100,000 + $600,000 + $30,000 = $730,000.

*Company has no management system standards. Savings will be less if the company has already implemented one or more management systems.

These savings are only for one site; how much more is it for an enterprise with multiple sites? More on this in the next chapter.

Organization of the Remaining Chapters (If You Missed It From the Preface)

This book introduces integrated management systems (IMS) in Chapter 1. Generally, speaking, integrated management systems mean integrated processes that satisfy quality management systems, environmental management systems, health and safety management systems, or food safety management systems (QMS, EMS, OHSMS, and/or FSMS). The authors define integrated management systems in one site as integrated processes, integrated risk, and integrated audits. Fundamental ideas and definitions of IMS are introduced in Chapter 1.

In Chapter 2, the IMS in one site will be extended to the enterprise with the ideas of integration and standardization for processes, risks, and audits. Fundamental ideas of enterprise integration and standardization, along with definitions and cost savings, will be presented in Chapter 2.

In Chapters 3, 4, and 5 the book will explain in detail integration and standardization (that is, single site and enterprise implementations for processes, risk, and audits). Chapter 6 will describe the Best In Class implementations of IMS, which will be the third book in this series of books on integrated management systems.

Chapters 7, 8, 9, 10, and 11 will describe implementations conducted globally in Asia, Middle East, and USA/Europe in automotive, semiconductor/electronics, service, aerospace, and the Food Industry. Chapter 12 will describe an important class of software called EwIMS software. It is our opinion that it is next to impossible to implement integrated management systems without it.

Chapter 13 will take a critical looks at the Pros and Cons in each implementation and describe lessons learned from implementing IMS in a site and or an Enterprise.

Chapter 14 will describe how the authors integrate the clauses and requirements and what methodology or process we integrate it with.

2

Integration vs. Standardization—
Why We Need Both

The last chapter covered the aspects of integration of management systems within one site. Integration was explained as involving uniformity of processes, risk, and audits. Integration can reduce management systems implementation costs by 50% and maintenance costs by 66%. While there are savings for each site of an enterprise to conduct stand-alone integration, the savings multiplies when it is standardized between the sites of the enterprise. This chapter will extend the definition of IMS in one site to that of an enterprise with multiple sites. This chapter will discuss integration and standardization, otherwise called enterprise integration, which includes integrated processes, risk, and audits across all facets of an enterprise.

In an enterprise of four sites with three management systems, simple math of 12 individual management systems vs. one integrated management system shows that if there are 500 documents on average in each of the systems, then there are 6000 documents in 12 management systems vs. 500 in one management system. If there are 100 process owners in one system, it equates to 1200 process owners in the four sites, each carrying out specific tasks assigned to them vs. 100 process owners carrying out globally assigned processes. Just the magnitude of extra work of 1200 processes vs. 100 global processes should explain the efficacy of integration and standardization. Twelve hundred processes and 1200 process owners are 12 times more likely to have failures than 100 processes with 100 process owners.

In this chapter we will also make the argument that after one site is integrated, the savings to the next site and the next is more than 50% for implementation and 66% for maintenance. We will develop this discussion later in the chapter.

When discussing standardization, we are discussing multiple plants in an enterprise. We see the same figure from Chapter 1 (Figure 2.1) that shows multiple design centers, plants, and warehouses.

In Chapter 1 we discussed how one plant can have stand-alone or integrated systems. How about an enterprise? How do we measure how standardized an enterprise is? Similar to integration, standardization of an enterprise can be measured by standardized processes, risk management, and audits.

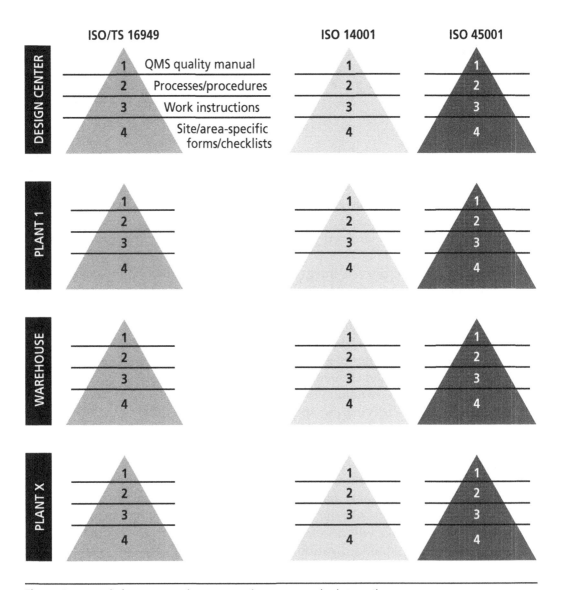

Figure 2.1 Stand-alone systems in an enterprise vs. enterprise integration.

INTEGRATED PROCESSES—ENTERPRISE

Each design center, warehouse, or plant can have implemented an integrated management system in its facility. They do not necessarily have to be standardized between locations. Standardization is not about common processes between QMS, EMS, and OHSMS in one site, but common approaches to processes (for example, document control and records control) globally in every site of the enterprise. In other words, integration is about common processes between the sites in an enterprise.

Key questions to ask for integrated processes:

a. Have you developed a management system integrating QMS, EMS, OHSMS, and other management systems for at least one site? If the organization has not done this, then this is the first step to standardization.

b. Does the organization have one manual for the entire corporation?

c. What percent of the processes and/or procedures of the organization are common?

d. What percent of the work instructions of the organization are common?

e. What percent of the forms and checklists of the organization are common?

f. Are there global process measures?

g. Are there global process owners?

STANDARDIZATION OF MANAGEMENT SYSTEMS

Let us consider an organization with multiple sites. For this example let us consider a corporate site, a plant, and a design center. Let us consider that the management system in this enterprise consists of six processes. Let us also consider that they have implemented QMS, EMS, and OHSMS management systems. See Table 2.1.

In this example, each of the sites has 100% integrated processes. In other words, they have integrated QMS, EMS, and OHSMS in their process documentation in each site. How do the sites relate to each other? Are they standardized? In other words, are there common processes between the sites? Sites 1 and 2 are 100% standardized, but site 3 has only standardized 66%. Enterprise standardization overall is 16/18 or 88.9%.

In calculating enterprise integration, the site integration will be calculated first and then the enterprise integration.

Table 2.1 Enterprise process score.

Site	Corporate	Plant	Design Center
Process Integration	6 processes	All are common with Corporate (100%)	4 common processes (4/6 or 66%)
Overall Enterprise Process Score	16/18 or 89%		

Process Standardization in an Enterprise

Each site in an enterprise has to score between 70% and 95% integration; then the total integration for the matrix is calculated to come up with one score for process standardization for the enterprise.

Enterprise processes are defined as management systems (processes) that score 70% to 100% for both process and process owner integration using an integration matrix for all sites (as shown in Table 2.1).

Integrated Risk Management—Enterprise

Enterprise risk management is the second element of a standardized enterprise. Enterprise risk management considers what process, product, or event has the highest risk in the enterprise. How is it controlled? Is the risk managed? This is something that top management should be aware of. Similar to Sarbanes-Oxley, these high-risk items need to have mock tests to ensure that the controls are working.

What must take place in an organization before risk can be evaluated and compared between quality, environmental, health and safety, and projects? The company should adopt a common risk methodology for quality, environmental, and health/safety. Even before that we could argue that the company needs to come to the understanding that risk is always defined as severity x occurrence. Also, that risk must be calculated first without any controls in place, so that the organization can understand what the highest risk items are. After that, controls are put in place.

Controls can be focused on either prevention or detection. Prevention controls eliminate or mitigate the cause of the risk, thus reducing the occurrence value. Detection controls identify when a cause or failure mode has occurred. The residual risk is calculated as severity x occurrence x detection.

A common risk methodology is not enough; the risk methodology must compare risk tables between the sites in the enterprise for severity, occurrence, and detection. Each can be used in tables with standardized scores (typically 1 to 10). In other words, 10 typically could mean death or insolvency of the business and 1 would mean negligible risk. This standardization of tables is essential if the risk numbers are to make any sense. In order to compare risk between quality, projects, environmental, financial, or health, it's necessary to use the same methodology and standardization of risk tables.

Once common methodology and index tables are used, the organization can develop standard risk templates (see Table 2.2). Risk templates are a library of risks for events, products, and processes that can be used again and again. Of course, a team can question any of the allocated risk numbers and adopt their own or have it globally changed. However, to be able to compare risk globally, risk templates ensure standardization of risk ratings.

Table 2.2 Standardized enterprise risk matrix example.

Corporate		Plant		Design Center	
Risk Methodology	FMEA	Risk Methodology	No Common Method	Risk Methodology	No Common Method
Risk Tables	Sev, Occ, and Det	Risk Tables	Unique Risk Tables	Risk Tables	No Common Tables
Common Risk Templates	Templates Created, Not Shared	No	No Templates	No	No Templates
Integration			0%		0%

Here are some common questions that can be asked to understand enterprise risk:

- Does each site of the enterprise have integrated risk in place (as in the previous chapter)? If not, this should be addressed first.
- Are common risk methodologies used between the sites?
- Do the sites use a common severity, occurrence, and detection table?
- Does the organization have a risk template for products, processes, and projects? Or do they create one every time a new product, process, or project is launched?

In this organization with three sites, there is no standardized enterprise risk management system. Only the corporate site has integrated the risk (created templates), but every other site uses or has implemented different systems. The enterprise scores a zero.

Integrated Risk—Enterprise

Integrated risk in an enterprise is defined as the use of common risk methodology, risk tables, and risk templates in the entire enterprise for quality, projects, environmental, health, safety, or food safety management systems. Common risk tables refer to comparable severity, occurrence, and detection tables enterprise wide. Standardized risk templates refer to the common treatment for the same potential events as it relates to quality, projects, environmental, health, safety, or food safety management systems risks.

INTEGRATED AUDITS—ENTERPRISE

This is the third element of standardized enterprises. Enterprise audits use the same audit schedule, auditors, and checklist across the sites of an organization. Standardization can include audit duration and the forms used across the enterprise (see Table 2.3). Integrated and standardized processes allow the organization to compare the robustness of processes, products, and systems. Furthermore, nonconformance rating scores between management systems and sites have much more validity using a standardized process.

Here are some common questions that could be asked to ascertain effectiveness of an enterprise audit:

- Do the individual sites in the enterprise have integrated systems? If not, this is the first step towards an enterprise audit.

- Do all the sites share the same audit process?

- Do all the sites have the same schedule, common checklists, and auditors?

- Is there a process to assure consistency of auditing among the sites?

In this example of three sites, the enterprise is integrated 66%. Similar to integrated audits, the benefit to the organization of enterprise audits occurs only when the processes are integrated. The integration score is the smaller of the enterprise process score and the enterprise audit score. In this example the enterprise process score is 89% and the enterprise audit score is 66%, hence the enterprise audit score is 66%.

Table 2.3 Standardized enterprise audits.

Site	Corporate	Plant	Design Center	Overall Score
Audit Process	SOP 22 – Internal Audit	Common	Unique	
Audit Schedule, Checklist, and Auditors	NA	Common	Unique	
Integration		100%	0%	66% (2/3)

Integration and Standardization Costs

Integrated management system savings are 50% for implementation,* 66% for maintenance, and 20% for third-party audits.

Integration and standardization result in 75% savings for implementation** (for all sites after the first site), and 85% for maintenance.** Reduction in third-party costs for multiple sites will be 20% of the third-party audit costs.

*The effort of implementing QMS, EMS and OHSMS (as a stand alone) is reduced to one combined implementation where all three standards are integrated. If implementation is considered 100% then a combined implementation could be considered 1/3 of the overall effort or 33% of the overall standalone effort. However, an integrated effort is a little more than 1/3 of the effort, hence the 50% figure is conservatively chosen.

**The savings from standardization results in the adoption of the integrated processes from site 1 to the other sites. There is no need to write documentation, the integrated documentation needs to be implemented. Hence, costs of implementation reduce dramatically since the number of processes and process owners do not change. However, management review and internal audits need to be conducted in each site.

Note: The savings for implementation is based on an organization having no systems. Adjustments will need to be made if one or more systems have been implemented.

Savings from Integration for One Site

Assumptions: Cost of implementation of three management system standards, $200,000; maintenance costs, $90,000/year; and third-party auditing costs, $45,000 for three years.

Savings from implementation (one-time cost): $200,000 x .50 = $100,000.

Savings from maintenance: $90,000 x .66 = $60,000 per year at each site; NPV at 10% would be $600,000. Maintenance includes maintaining stand alone processes of QMS, EMS and OHSAS, which will be combined to 1/3 of the previous total with 1/3 less process owners. Management reviews and internal audits will be 1/3 lower as well. Hence, maintenance of the QMS, EMS and OHSAS will be reduced to 33% of the previous costs each year.

(continued)

Savings from Integration for One Site *(continued)*

Savings from third-party audit costs: $1500 each year x .20; NPV is $30,000.
20% of the third-party audit costs: the reduction is provided by registrars is for integrated audits. Up to 40% is allowed for organizations with more than 10 sites.

Total Savings: $100,000 + $600,000 + $30,000 = $730,000.

*Company has no management system standards. Savings will not be the same if there are some costs for existing systems.

These savings are only for one site.

SUMMARY

In our example, the enterprise with three sites (corporate, plant and design center) scores 89% for process, 0% for risk and 66% for audit (see Table 2.4). If we assume that the three sites are of the same size, then the savings numbers calculated for integration would apply to each of the sites. In other words, the savings from integration would be roughly $730,000 for each site or $2.19 million for all three sites. (These savings resulted from the savings attributed to implementing systems, which was 50%, and savings from maintaining the systems, which was 66%. See shaded boxes above.)

How much additional savings do we get from a standardized enterprise? Standardizing the enterprise would result in saving an *additional 25%* of implementation costs, an *additional 20%* in maintenance costs, and an *additional 20%* of integrated registrar audits costs. In other words, integration and standardization will result in a 75% savings in implementation in all additional sites (after the first site is integrated), 85% in savings in maintenance costs, and 20% reduction for multiple sites (the savings will increase to 40% if there are more than 10 sites).

Table 2.4 Enterprise process score.

Site	Corporate	Plant	Design Center
Process Integration	6 Processes	Common (100%)	4 Common Processes (4/6 or 66%)
Overall Enterprise Process Score	16/18 or 89%		

Standardized Enterprise Risk

In this organization with three sites, there is no standardized enterprise risk management system (Figure 2.5). The corporate site has integrated the risk, but the other sites have different systems. The enterprise scores a zero.

In this example, each of the sites has 100% integrated processes. In other words, each site has integrated QMS, EMS, and OHSMS in its process documentation.

How do the sites relate to each other? Are they standardized? In other words, how well has the enterprise integrated? Sites 1 and 2 are 100% standardized, but site 3 has only standardized 66%. Enterprise standardization overall is 16/18 or 88.9%.

Standardized Enterprise Audits

In this example of three sites (Table 2.6), the enterprise is integrated 66%. Similar to integrated audits, the benefit to the organization of enterprise audits is only there if the processes are integrated. The integration score is the smaller of the enterprise process score and the enterprise audit score. In this example the enterprise process score is 89% and the enterprise audit score is 66%, hence the enterprise audit score is 66%.

Table 2.5 Standardized enterprise risk.

Corporate		Plant		Design Center	
Risk Methodology	FMEA	Risk Methodology	No Common Method	Risk Methodology	No Common Method
Risk Tables	Sev, Occ, and Det	Risk Tables	Unique Risk Tables	Risk Tables	No Common Tables
Common Risk Templates	Templates Created, Not Shared	No	No Templates	Team	No Templates
Integration			0%		0%

Table 2.6 Standardized enterprise audit of three sites.

Site	Corporate	Plant	Design Center	Overall Score
Audit Process	SOP 22 – Internal Audit	Common	Unique	
Audit Schedule, Checklist, and Auditors	NA	Common	Unique	
Integration		100%	0%	66% (2/3)

Site	Enterprise
Enterprise Process	89%
Enterprise Risk	0%
Enterprise Audit	66%
Overall Enterprise Score	89/0/66

In this enterprise including a corporate location, one plant, and a design center, there is not enough enterprise integration. The enterprise score is 89/0/66 (a perfect score is 100/100/100). There are two potential savings in an enterprise— first, that each site is integrated and second, that there is enterprise integration. The savings from site integration is $2.19 million for all three sites.

Calculating Savings for An Enterprise

Using the same numbers as found in Chapter 1, let us assume that the per-site cost for implementing three management systems is $200,000, the cost to maintain all three non-integrated systems is $90,000, and third-party auditing cost for a three-year period is $45,000.

Savings in implementation costs for each site after the first one: $200,000 x .75 = $150,000 for each of the two remaining sites, or $300,000 for both of the sites.

Note: The savings for the first site is the savings from integration (that is, $200,000 x .50 = $100,000).

Total savings in implementation is $400,000.

Savings in maintenance costs per year: $90,000 costs for each site x .85 = $76,500 for one site or $229,500 per year for all three sites. NPV at 10% interest is $2,295,000 for all three sites.

Savings in third-party audit costs for three years: $45,000 x .20 = $9,000 for one site for three years or $27,000 for all three sites for three years. Savings in one year for all three sites is $9,000. NPV at 10% Interest is $90,000 for three sites.

There is an additional savings from doing integrated risk or using one methodology and reusing risk scores between sites. If we assume each site spends $50,000 each year to calculate risk for new products and processes, then the cost is $150,000 for the three sites and the NPV for integrated risk at 10% interest is $1.5 million.

Grand total for all three sites for integration and standardization is $400,000 from implementation plus $2,295,000 for maintenance plus $90,000 for third-party auditing, or $2,785,000 for three sites. When we include the integrated risk, savings increase to $4.285 million.

Integration and standardization will result in a 75% savings in implementation in all additional sites (after the first site is integrated), 85% savings in maintenance costs, and 20% reduction in third-party audit costs in each site and an additional 40% reduction for multiple sites (if there are more than ten sites). The savings from site integration and enterprise integration is $2.8 million. There is a savings in integrated risk that has not been accounted for, savings generated by reusing the risks scores developed in one site into the other sites. This integrated risk score is reused in products, processes, projects, changes, and any other risk calculation for quality, projects, environmental, and health and safety. We will discuss integrated risk more in Chapter 4. Taking New Product Introduction for a family of products and processes, we can imagine that the cost for risk evaluation is $200,000. In organizations that conduct this risk evaluation, risk is evaluated using Systems and Design Failure Modes and Effects Analysis, Process Failure Mode and Effects Analysis, Capability Studies, Control Plans, and many other documents before product is released. If an enterprise averages one new product launch every year and the risk evaluation costs are $150,000, then there is a savings in present value costs using the same 10% discounted value of $1.5 million.

In short, enterprise integration results in a total of $4.3 million in savings. In other words, both site integration described in the first chapter and enterprise integration described in this chapter maximizes the savings potential of the organization. Astute readers will understand that the actual savings are much more than that described in these two chapters.

3

Integrating Processes between QMS, EMS, OHSMS, FSMS

In this chapter we will explore the specifics of the integration of processes within one site and then look at integration enterprise wide. We discussed the motivation for this in the introduction to Chapter 2, using as an example an enterprise with three sites and three management systems of QMS, EMS, and OHSMS. We said that the simple math of 12 individual management systems versus one integrated management system easily explained the benefit (see Figure 3.1). Further we explained that the nine management systems (if there were an average of 100 processes and process owners in a system) equated to 1200 processes and process owners versus 100 processes and process owners when the enterprise integrated into one management system. The savings numbers from the last chapter do not fully explain the gains of efficiency and simplification that take place (soft savings versus hard savings) with site and enterprise integration.

INTEGRATION WITHIN ONE SITE

An apex document for a standard is one that provides the organization's foundations for that standard. It would include a policy statement and scope as related to the standard's focus. Even though the apex document of a documented management system can be integrated, very little savings ensue from this integration. The organization could document a manual for each of the standards or integrate them into one single manual. The quality manual was a requirement of QMS standards until the advent of ISO 9001:2015. With the latest revision of ISO 9001, there are no more requirements for quality manuals or documented procedures. Although not required by the standards, when skillfully designed, the apex document explains how the organization satisfies a particular standard and it is also a pointer into the integrated management system. Generally speaking, manuals should be less than 15 pages long and should show how QMS, EMS, OHSMS, or FSMS requirements are satisfied by the integrated management system. It should also have a matrix of requirements/processes to level II and III documentation. Integration of the processes, work instructions, and forms/checklists is where the integration effort should be focused (see the process map example in Figure 3.2).

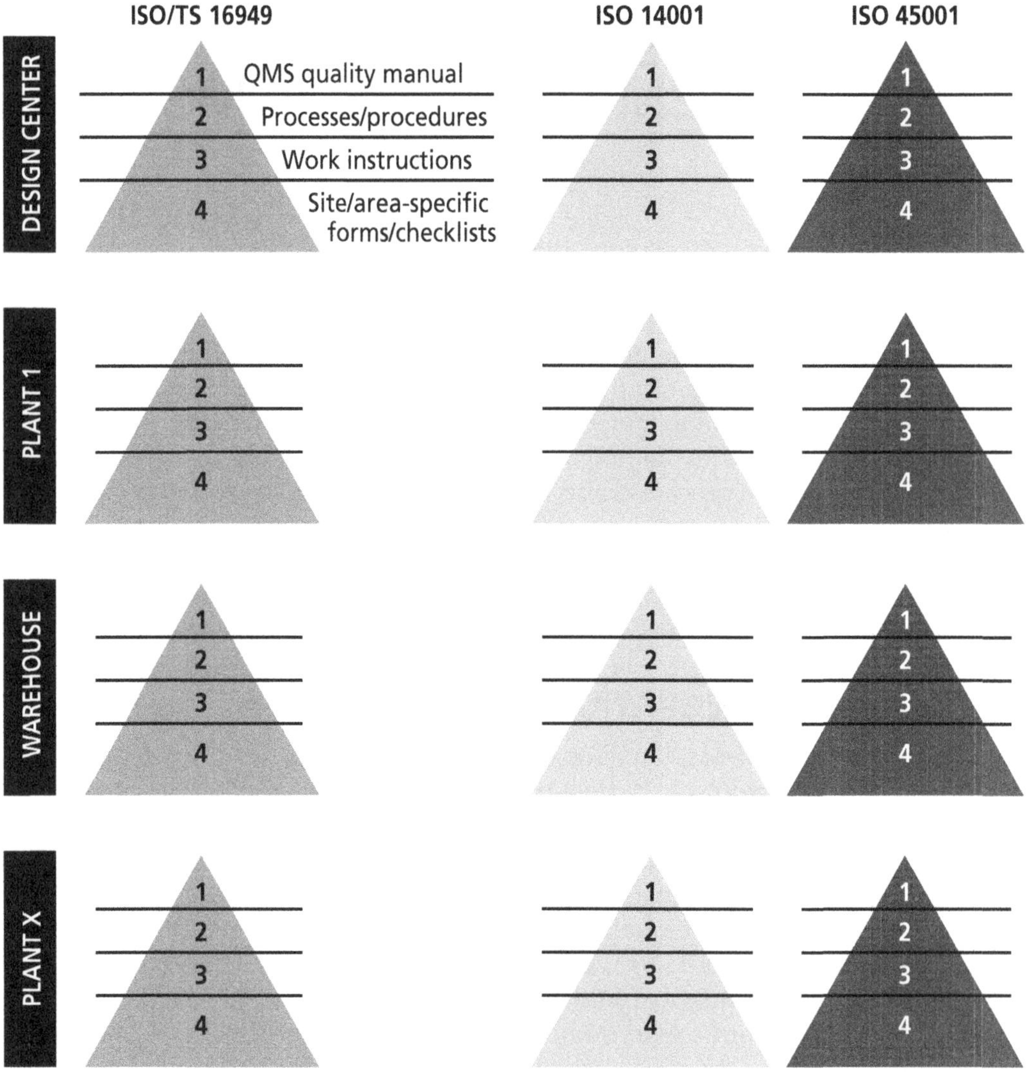

Figure 3.1 No integration or standardization.

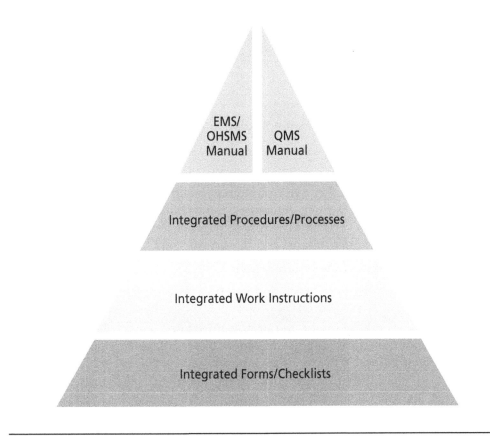

Figure 3.2 Stand-alone system (one site).

DESIGNING THE MANUAL (APEX DOCUMENT)—LEVEL I

For integration purposes it is good to have a common manual for QMS, EMS, OHSMS, and a FSMS (as applicable). The manual can be thought of as a document that explains the integration as well as a tool to describe the organization's system to its customers. It should be short, well designed, and have the look and feel of a marketing document. It is the first document seen by customers and third parties and as such should leave the viewer with a positive opinion of the company. Below is a list of topics that can be included in a business management systems (BMS) manual. It should be designed to be an active and useful document, with yearly updates that communicate management system policies, changes, mission/vision, KPIs, and key initiatives.

Note: The process map of the ISO 9001 QMS reflects the processes of the entire organization including new product development, sales, purchasing, and top management processes. As such it encompasses the entire business and is not just about the quality department. To ensure this understanding, the authors have always called the QMS apex document a BMS or policy manual. With the integration of the environmental, health and safety, and food safety requirements, the management system becomes even more of a business management system, or BMS. Hence the name BMS Manual for the apex document and the name BMS to reflect the entire system.

BMS Manual Table of Contents

1. Introduction to the Management System and the Organization's History
2. Organization's Products, Locations, and Markets
3. Scope of the BMS
   a. The scope of the quality, environmental, health and safety and food safety (Q, E, HS, FS) management systems should be the same. It should identify the standards and the respective revision levels, organizational entities with enough details, and the products included in the BMS.
4. Mission and Vision of the organization
5. Quality, Environmental, Health and Safety and Food Safety (Q,E,HS, FS) Policies
   a. The policies can be integrated or non-integrated. At this time, we feel it is prudent to allow top management to articulate the policy of the organization for Q, E, HS, or FS separately.
6. Process Map—Integrated Process Map (for QMS, EMS, and OHSMS). The processes specific to quality, environmental or health/safety can be color coded.
7. Process List and Process Metrics
   a. Omnex provides a document called a BMS control plan to document the processes, the process metrics, person responsible, acceptance criteria, and control method.
8. Business Key Indicators
   a. The business indicators, sometimes called KPI (key performance indicators) or key measurables (Ford QOS) or business metrics, all articulate the metrics measured at the top of the organization. The KPIs should aggregate and disaggregate up and down the organization. The top level indicators or KPIs should include Q, E, HS and FS metrics along with the other KPIs of the organization. The review of the business key indicators should result in the management review requirements of the organization being fulfilled.
   b. Best in Class implementation of the key indicators is to implement it following the BOS Process that Omnex wrote for Ford Motor Company in 1993 and implemented widely afterwards. See Alignment Chart of the BOS that aligns the needs and expectations of interested parties (9.2 in ISO 9001:2015) with Objectives (6.2 in ISO 9001:2015) and Management Reviews (9.3 in ISO 9001:2015). The BOS uses Trend Charts with Goal Lines, Paretos, and Action Plan reports. The action

plan reports provides a summary of activities of the Organizations initiatives to close the gap from where the trend line is today and where they want to go ie. the goal line. Note: Ford called this process a Quality Operating System or QOS.

9. Organization's Key Initiatives for the Year
   a. The key initiatives of the organization reflects the continuous improvement activities to close the gap in the key indicators and the respective goals established.

10. Explanation of the Key Features of the BMS
    a. This section explains the BMS including the methodologies adopted by the organization to satisfy the Q, E, HS, and/or FSMS requirements.

11. Standardized Management Meetings for the Enterprise
    a. This section of the manual will describe key meetings held in each entity of the organization, its recommended duration and frequency, and the agenda items it needs to cover. More meetings can be held, but it describes how the organization functions in managing its operations.

This manual can be designed from its inception to be a manual for the entire enterprise.

The QMS can be used as the base for building the integration. This is not necessary, but the QMS is typically the first standard that most organizations implement. Note, some food organizations may start with an FSMS, and integration could start with an FSMS also. However, in this chapter we will focus on QMS as the basis of the integration. We are not purposely qualifying the QMS, as they come in many flavors including ISO 9001:2008, AS9100, Rev C, or ISO/TS 16949. The processes we will discuss are therein all the different types of QMS.

PROCESS APPROACH, THE KEY TO INTEGRATION—LEVEL II

The first place for integration is the process map (process approach) of QMS as required in Clause 4.1. Processes are the building blocks of integration. See Figure 3.3 for an example.

Each of the processes in the process map must satisfy multiple requirements of QMS, EMS, OHSMS, and FSMS (if applicable). The matrix below has been designed with the intent of integrating processes. Due to the high level structure change (HLS), the standards fundamentally align. ISO 9001, ISO 14001, and ISO 45001 follow this new HLS as show below. The commonality of the requirements in each of the sections between the three standards is an important consideration for integration. A comparison of requirements in 5.1 Leadership and Commitment between ISO 9001 and ISO 14001 showed an almost 100% agreement between both standards. A comparison with ISO 45001 showed commonality as well as a few additional requirements. However, it is worth nothing that the ISO 45001 is still a committee draft at the time of this writing.

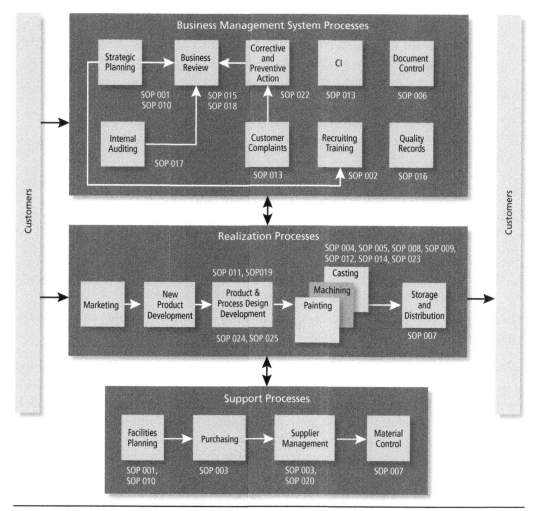

Figure 3.3 Process map example.

A comparison of Clause 9.2 Internal audit between all three standards shows an almost 100% agreement between all three standards. See Chapter 14 for more comparison of each standard.

High Level Structure—All new standards need to follow this structure. The new ISO 9001, ISO 14001, and ISO 45001 follow this high level structure:

1. Scope

2. Normative References

3. Terms and Definitions

4. Context of the Organization
   - Understanding the Organization and its Context
   - Needs and Expectations
   - Scope
   - Management System
5. Leadership
   - Management Commitment
   - Policy
   - Roles, Responsibility and Authority
6. Planning
   - Actions to Address Risks and Opportunities
   - Objectives and Plans to Achieve Them
7. Support
   - Resources
   - Competence
   - Awareness
   - Communication
   - Documented Information
8. Operation
   - Operational Planning and Control
9. Performance Evaluation
   - Monitoring, Measurement, Analysis and Evaluation
   - Internal Audit
   - Management Review
10. Improvement
   - Nonconformity and Corrective Action
   - Continual Improvement

Chapter 14 compares the requirements in the standard. It shows that more than 95% of the requirements are common between the different standards including QMS, EMS, OHSMS standards. In many cases the process can be the same, but the scope of the process has to be enlarged to include the broader topic of environmental or health and safety. For example, if a document control process for QMS addressed only the quality documents, this same process could address with a change of scope the EMS, OHSMS, and FSMS documents. See box showing how a document control process for a QMS (in this example for Omnex) can be edited to become an IMS process.

Document Control for Quality Management Systems

1.0 Purpose:
To define the process used to control documents important to the quality system.

2.0 Scope:
All documents related to the quality system.

3.0 Responsibilities:
All Omnex personnel who create or maintain quality documents.

4.0 Definitions:
A level I document is part of the QMS manual. A level II document is a procedure. A Level III document is a work instruction. A level IV document is a form, tag, checklist, or similar.

5.0 Procedure:

5.1 Quality Management System Documentation

5.1.1 All level I-IV documents are controlled using the document control software Document Pro®. Any documents may be created using Microsoft Office or other programs until they are submitted into Document Pro for approval. Training documents may be in any software program.

5.1.2 The Management Representative will establish approvals for each new or changed document in Document Pro. Document Pro will then handle control of approvals automatically. The person most closely associated with the process will normally write documents. They are reviewed by a higher-level manager, and approved by the Management Representative or designated Leadership Team member.

5.1.3 All requests for changes to quality documents shall be requested through Document Pro. Any personnel with access to Document Pro can request such a change.

5.2 Documents of External Origin

5.2.1 Electronic copies of documents of external origin requiring control are controlled in Document Pro in the same fashion as QMS documents in "Referenced Documents-Controlled." Upon receipt of any documents of external origin, the office staff posts the document to Doc Pro and notifies all staff via affected email.

5.2.2 The office staff maintains paper copies of documents of external origin requiring control for training or reference purposes.

5.2.3 As a matter of policy, Omnex respects the rights of owners of all copyrighted materials. When considering use of any published materials from sources other than Omnex, it is the responsibility of the Product Champion to determine whether permission is required. Use includes incorporation into published training materials, presentation in seminars, reproduction, translation and/or distribution. For guidance, refer to RDC 010: University of Texas Fair Use Statement in Omnex.EwQMS.com.; reference documents

Document Control for Integrated Management System (Quality, Environmental, and Health and Safety Management Systems)

1.0 Purpose:
To define the process used to control documents important to the quality, environmental, and health/safety systems.

2.0 Scope:
All documents related to the quality, environmental, and health and safety management systems.

3.0 Responsibilities:
All Omnex personnel who create or maintain quality, environmental, and health and safety documents.

4.0 Definitions:
A level I document is a part of the Manual. A level II document is a procedure or a process. A Level III document is a work instruction. A level IV document is a form, tag, checklist or similar.

5.0 Procedure:

5.1 Integrated Management System Documentation

5.1.1 All level I-IV documents are controlled in Document Pro. Any documents may be created using Microsoft Office or other programs until they are submitted into Document Pro for approval. Training documents may be in any software program.

5.1.2 The Management Representative will establish approvals for each new or changed document in Document Pro. Document Pro will then handle control of approvals automatically. The person most closely associated with the process will normally write documents. They are reviewed by a higher-level manager, and approved by the Management Representative or designated Leadership Team member.

5.1.3 All requests for changes to documents shall be requested through Document Pro. Any personnel with access to Document Pro can request such a change.

5.2 Documents of External Origin

5.2.1 Electronic copies of documents of external origin requiring control are controlled in Document Pro in the same fashion as QMS documents in "Referenced Documents-Controlled." Upon receipt of any documents of external origin, the office staff posts the document to Doc Pro and notifies all staff via affected email.

5.2.2 The office staff maintains paper copies of documents of external origin requiring control for training or reference purposes.

5.2.3 As a matter of policy, Omnex respects the rights of owners of all copyrighted materials. When considering use of any published materials from sources other than Omnex, it is the responsibility of the Product Champion to determine whether permission is required. Use includes incorporation into published training materials, presentation in seminars, reproduction, translation and/or distribution. For guidance, refer to RDC 010: University of Texas Fair Use Statement in Omnex.EwQMS.com; reference documents.

It won't take much time to update documents for integrated management systems. In this actual Omnex quality management system document example, the title of the procedure and scope were updated. References to quality were expanded to include quality, environmental, and health and safety. The edit of the documentation was easy, but how about the implementation?

For implementation purposes, Doc Pro should be able to input all the QMS, EMS, and OHSMS documents. Next routings for approvals need to be possible for the IMS, QMS, EMS, and OHSMS documents. Lastly, Doc Pro should be available for everyone who needs access to it. In this example the creation of an integrated document was easy, but the time consuming change will be to move all of the documents in to the same document management tool and process. Let us look at a second example of a strategic planning process next.

Business Planning Process

A process for setting yearly objectives and the management review (called the business planning process), on the other hand, can be more complex. The same procedure may be used, but the process of updating the business objectives would need to be broadened to include Q, E, HS, and FSMS (if it applies) topics, which then needs to be included in the management review. The business review needs to include all the topics of the Q, E, HS, and FSMS management reviews. A rough count of the three standards—ISO 9001, ISO 14001 and ISO 45001—that are in the process of being updated show that the management reviews have 31 items to be reviewed. These items can be consolidated to seven as shown in the management review topics matrix (Table 3.1).

Integrating processes need not be a simple scope extension of the process. As the business planning process shows, it could entail getting agreement between various functions. First, the organization's management review process participants need to agree that they will integrate the quality, environmental, health and safety, and food safety objectives into one set of business objectives (these topics will be referred to as Q, E, HS, and FS (as applicable) going forward). Next, they need to agree that the business review is indeed the management review and that this process should encompass all the reviews required by the different standards. See the appendix of this chapter for the strategic planning process for QMS and IMS. The changes are shaded so it is easy to see the difference between QMS and IMS documents.

In this manner, each process in the integrated management system should be designed by cross-functional teams.

Table 3.1 Management review topics matrix.

	ISO 9001 DIS	ISO 14001 DIS	ISO 45001 CD1
Inputs	Status of actions from previous releases	Status of actions from previous releases	Status of actions from previous releases
	Changes in external and internal issues	Changes in external and internal issues	Changes in external and internal issues
		Aspects and risks updated	
	Information on the performance (7 items)	Information on the performance (4 items)	Information on the performance (7 items)
		Communication to external parties	Policy and objectives met
		Opportunities for continual improvement	Opportunities for continual improvement
		Adequacy of resources	Adequacy of resources
Outputs/Decisions Related To	Continual improvement opportunities	Continual improvement opportunities	Continual improvement opportunities
	Changes needed	Changes needed	Changes needed
		Suitability and adequacy	
		Objectives not met	
		Implications for strategic decisions	

DEVELOPING INTEGRATED MANAGEMENT SYSTEMS PROCEDURES—LEVEL II

In order to integrate procedures it's necessary to follow these steps:

a. Identify the process map of the organization. Ensure that it truly represents the organization's processes and is not modeled after the clauses of the standard. If the process documentation in an organization only has QMS, EMS, OHSMS, or FSMS requirements or clause names as processes, it's possible that the process design was modeled after the standard and the process map would be called a "clause oriented" process map design. The process "sequencing and interaction" should follow how each organization actually works, not how the standard is organized. In such cases the process map would most probably need to be redesigned.

A well designed process map would connect and cut across sales, design, manufacturing, and warehouses—all the entities in an enterprise—whether they are in United States, Europe, or Asia.

b. List the QMS processes and the clauses they satisfy in a process integration matrix as shown below in Table 3.2. This matrix clearly identifies the clauses of each standard that each process conforms to. The cross-functional team identified below must ensure that the process conforms to these clause requirements. Note, in this example, that the matrix is populated with the processes from the process map shown earlier in Figure 3.2.

c. Create cross-functional teams of Q, E, HS, and FSMS personnel and designate an enterprise process owner. These teams will meet either via web meetings or in person to redesign enterprise processes.

Cross-functional teams work to enlarge the scope of the process or to redesign processes to satisfy all the "shalls" of each of the standards under consideration—QMS, EMS, OHSMS, or FSMS.

d. Identify process measures. Update the BMS control plan with the process measures. See BMS control plan in Figure 3.4.

e. Identify process owners at each site. These process owners will be responsible to comment on and to implement these processes.

Table 3.2 Process integration matrix.
Note: This process list is only an example.

Process Name	QMS, EMS, and OHSMS
Strategic Planning	4.1 Understanding the Organization and its Context 5.1 Leadership and Commitment 5.2 Policy 6.2 Objectives and Planning to Achieve Them
Determining Customer / Interested Party Expectations	4.2 Needs and Expectations of Interested Parties 5.1.2 Customer Focus
Business Review	9.3 Management Review
Internal Auditing	9.2 Internal Audit 9.1.2 Evaluation of Compliance (EMS & OHSMS)
Corrective and Preventive Actions	10.2 Nonconformity and Corrective Action
Customer Complaints	8.2.1 Customer Communication
Continual Improvement	10.3 Continual Improvement
Document Control	7.5 Documented Information
Quality Records	7.5 Documented Information
Recruiting and Training	7.1.2 People 7.2 Competence 7.3 Awareness
Marketing	7.4 Communication
New Product Development	8.2 Determination of Requirements of Products and Services
Risk Identification Prioritization	6.1 Opportunities to Address Risks and Opportunities
Manage the Change	6.3 Planning of Changes
Managing Organizational Knowledge	7.1.6 Organizational Knowledge 8.5.6 Control of Changes
Process Control	4.4 Quality Management System and its Processes 8.1 Operational Planning and Control
Storage and Distribution	4.4 Quality Management System and its Processes 8.1 Operational Planning and Control 8.5.4 Preservation (QMS only)
Facilities Planning	4.4 Quality Management System and its Processes 8.1 Operational Planning and Control 7.1.3 Infrastructure (QMS only)
Purchasing	8.4 Control of Externally Provided Products and Services
Material Control	8.5.2 Identification and Traceability (QMS only) 8.5.3 Property Belonging to Customers or External Parties (QMS only) 8.6 Release of Products and Services
Manufacturing Process Control	8.5.1 Control of Production and Service Provision (QMS only)
Post-delivery Processes	8.5.5 Post-delivery Activities
Control of Nonconforming	8.7 Control of Nonconforming Process Outputs, Products and Services

Process Activity	Customer Req/ Expectation	Key Process/ COP	Measurement	Responsibility	Acceptance Criteria 2002 Q1, Q2, Q3, Q4	Review Frequency	Control Methods	Comments/ Reaction
				EXAMPLES				
Business Fulfillment	On-time delivery	K	% on-time in operations	Logistics	94, 95, 96, 96%	4/yr	Monthly management meeting	Corrective action after 3 consecutive
			% on-time to customer	Production control	100%	4/yr	Trend chart	C/A is more than 15% off target
Customer Complaint	Provide timely response	C	Complaint response	Quality	10 days	4/Yr	Production control dept	Continue to monitor
Design & Development	Meet timing requirement		Time to market	Design/dev	52 weeks	Weekly	Quality department	R, Y, G reaction
Business Creation	Innovation		Patents filed	Design	20 per year	Monthly	Design meeting	Continue to monitor

Business Management System Control Plan

Organization: _____

General Manager: _____

Product Description: _____

Issue/Rev Date: _____

Figure 3.4 BMS control plan.

Three books are planned in this series on integrated management systems, including *Integrated Management Systems Implementation, Integrated Management Systems Auditing,* and *Developing Best In Class Processes for Integrated Management Systems.* Designing effective and efficient enterprise process maps and processes will be the topic of the third book in this series.

DEVELOPING INTEGRATED MANAGEMENT SYSTEMS WORK INSTRUCTIONS—LEVEL III

Almost 80% of work instructions in an organization center on its manufacturing processes. Typically, each process will have work instructions, inspection sheets, preventative maintenance sheets, and setup instructions. When developing integrated level III documents, it should be understood that these are the control documents that ensure that quality, environmental, health and safety, and food safety controls are carried out on the shop floor. In other words, this same set of documents should allow for Q, E, HS, and FSMS controls on the manufacturing shop floor. Controls also have a relationship with risk evaluation. See Figure 3.5.

The relationship between risk evaluation and controls will be discussed in greater details in Chapter 4, Integrated Risk. Controls required for manufacturing processes are detailed in section 8.1 & 8.5.1 in ISO 9001:2015 and 8.1 in both EMS and OHSMS Operational Planning and Control, and HACCP in Food Safety Management Systems.

Integration and standardization of risk using product and process families is a topic of Chapter 4.

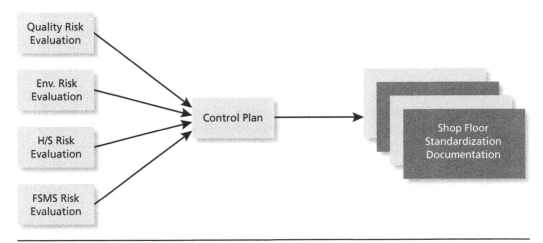

Figure 3.5 Controls–risk evaluation relationship.

DEVELOPING INTEGRATED MANAGEMENT SYSTEMS FORMS/CHECKLISTS—LEVEL IV

Forms and checklists are typically associated with process documentation. Once the processes are integrated, it is possible to modify them for use with Q, E, HS, and/or FSMS.

Integrated forms and checklists are an important part of integration. Further guidance is offered in book three of this series.

ENTERPRISE INTEGRATION

After the apex documents for level I and II have been integrated in one site, then the integrated documents can be flowed out to the organization in one of two ways. A dozen or so documents can be picked for initial standardization or all documents can be chosen. Here are the steps to follow:

1. Get top management commitment for enterprise integration. Explain the savings and benefits that come with integration. Explain how objections could come from many quarters and that their steady message must be to integrate. The implementers will make the determination if someone has a valid reason not to integrate. Top management must send a clear message that adopting global processes will require each organizational entity to make real changes in how it operates and conducts processes.

2. Determine whether to roll out all level II processes or to roll out specific level II processes to the entire organization as global processes. Some of the processes and/or documents include the following: common policy, objectives and business reviews, new product development, change management, process and operational controls, risk evaluation, document control, records control, internal audits, firing and competency management, new employee orientation, and others.

3. Determine global process owners and process measures.

4. Create cross-functional process groups for each process and hold meetings to determine changes that may be needed to create global processes. Implementers need to be receptive and open minded to make necessary changes. Note that process groups should include representatives from E, HS, and FS and several sites. It's not necessary to include representatives from every site, especially if this is an integration involving a large corporation.

5. Caution: Do not simplify process documentation by removing controls and details. Sometimes organizations attempt to integrate by removing details at level II and asking sites to add the details at level III, completely negating the purpose of process standardization and enterprise processes.

6. Implement the global processes.

7. Conduct internal audits to ensure processes are followed. Send global teams to audit each of the plants.

8. Conduct third-party audits to the integration and standardization processes. Negotiate reduced audit days and the savings that ensue.

SUMMARY

This chapter succinctly explains integration of the BMS and covers level I, II, III, and IV documentation. The authors bring global teams together for a two-day workshop and integrate multiple processes during the event. Instead of integrating in one site and then standardizing globally, which is one strategy, it is possible to directly move toward integration and standardization with a global team.

The focus on the BMS integration and standardization is the level I and level II integration covered in this chapter. This integration will bring in large returns to an enterprise. Level III strategies are covered, along with risk evaluation, management, and control. Level III control documents ensure a process operates with minimum risk to Q, E, HS, or FSMS. These operator communication documents should become part of training and visual instruction.

Top management commitment is an important ingredient for success. It is important that top management understand why they are integrating, and the benefits of integration. The authors' experience show that the best integrations take place when top management insists on one way to run the organization and when they require global processes with no variation between sites.

APPENDIX – BUSINESS PLANNING PROCESS*

The process below satisfies the requirements of 5.4 Planning and 5.6 Management Review in ISO 9001 and covers the 4.3.3 Objectives, Targets and Programs and 4.6 Management Review. The additions to satisfy EMS and OHSMS are shaded in the flow chart (see Figure 3A.1).

Escar Manufacturing Corporate Offices Detroit MI	BUSINESS PLANNING PROCESS	SOP-10 page 1 of 13 2014-12-23 Rev. B

Section 1. Purpose

1.1   This document outlines the business planning and review process for all Escar Manufacturing organizations.

1.2   The business planning process is a disciplined activity conducted to assure that customer and other stakeholder interests are included in organization business objectives and actions.

1.3   This document outlines business process continuous improvement practices.

Section 2. Scope

2.1   This document applies to all Escar Manufacturing Site Management Steering Committees (MSC).

Section 3. Applicable standards and specifications

3.1   ISO/TS 16949:2009, Quality management systems - Particular requirements for the application of ISO 9001:2008 for automotive production and relevant service part organizations

3.2   ISO 9001:2008, Quality management systems -Requirements

3.3   ISO 9004:2009, Quality Management Systems - Managing for the sustained success of an organization

3.4   ISO 14001: 2004, Environmental management systems – Requirements with guidance for use

3.5   OHSAS 18001:2007 Occupational Health and Safety Management Systems – Requirements

3.6   QSM 1, Business Management System, Escar Mfg.

3.7   SOP-18, Performance Metrics Review.

Section 4. General

4.1   An example of the annual business planning cycle is shown in Figure 3A.1.

* *Note: This procedure illustrates integrating standards using the previous version of ISO 9001, ISO 14001, and OHSAS 18001 (now ISO 45001).*

Section 5. Definitions

5.1   Vision Statement

    5.1.1   The organization vision is summarized in a statement that identifies the attainable objective for the organization. The vision acts as a focus reference point for the organization.

    5.1.2   The vision statement is aligned with and supports all Escar manufacturing sites. The vision statement is composed by the organization MSC.

    5.1.3   The vision statement is reviewed and revised during the annual business planning process, but may be revised as needed throughout the year. Changes to the vision may necessitate changes to the mission statement, strategic plan, or other documents.

5.2   Mission Statement

    5.2.1   The organization mission statement is implied by the vision; it identifies the key actions needed to achieve the vision. It is generated by the MSC; it is aligned with and supports the Escar mission statement.

    5.2.2   The mission statement is revised as indicated by modifications to the organization vision. It is reviewed annually by the MSC.

5.3   Organizational Objectives / Key Customer Expectations

    5.3.1   Key customer expectations are developed by the MSC. They are strongly linked to the organization mission statement.

    5.3.2   The organizational objectives are the identified proficiencies needed to achieve the mission and vision, as well as general business operational targets.

5.4   Key Performance Metrics

    5.4.1   Key performance metrics are measurable activities with a time horizon that indicate progress in support of the organization objectives/expectations, mission and vision.

    5.4.2   Performance metrics are linked to expectations / objectives and other business planning data.

5.5   Balanced Scorecard

    5.5.1   The balanced scorecard approach is used by the Organization to align objectives / expectations with metrics and to track performance to identified targets.

    5.5.2   The balanced scorecard is updated and formally reviewed at least quarterly, with an annual rollup review.

5.6   Operational Review Meeting

    5.6.1   Operational review meetings are held regularly to manage progress toward the goals of the organization.

Section 5. Definitions *(continued)*

    5.6.2 Review meeting results are reviewed and improvement actions are identified and tracked to completion in the meeting minutes.

    5.6.3 Review meeting actions are primarily intended to improve performance to the balanced scorecard and to the yearly operation plan to assure conformity with business objectives.

    5.6.4 Review meeting activity is part of and includes focus on continuous improvement of the organization's business processes.

5.7 Yearly Operating Plan

    5.7.1 The plan establishes financial performance targets. The financial forecast referenced in the operating plan financial measures is revised at least quarterly.

5.8 Strategic Plan

    5.8.1 The strategic plan is composed by the MSC utilizing inputs from customers, internal audits, personnel development plans and Organization employees and is presented to Escar's management.

    5.8.2 The distribution is controlled.

5.9 New Product Planning Team

    5.9.1 Product planning is typically performed by a combination of marketing, sales and engineering personnel, with consultation from design/development and other areas as required.

    5.9.2 This activity includes market, competitive, and technology analyses.

    5.9.3 It also includes maintaining and revising the Escar product mix throughout the year. The latest version, together with analysis data, is provided for the strategic planning activity.

    5.9.4 This team is responsible for defining specific new products. New product requests are submitted to the MSC for approval and then to design & development. This activity assures that Escar will continue to offer a competitive product portfolio in its chosen market.

Section 6. Business Planning Procedure

6.1 Inputs – The data below are used to support and refine the business planning process.

    6.1.1 Escar Manufacturing and the responsible site MSC provide top-down data for business planning, including the following:

- Escar Corporation and Site Vision and Mission Statements
- Business Environmental Conditions report
- Other stakeholder requirements and expectations

Section 6. Business Planning Procedure *(continued)*

6.1.2 The Organization Vision and Mission Statements and other inputs including:

- Year-end balanced scorecard and other self assessment results, together with identified improvement opportunities from operational review meeting activity

- Manufacturing capability and capacity requirements, along with historical performance results for each site

6.1.3 Customer requirements, such as on-time delivery, quality, ppm levels and customer satisfaction, such as responsiveness to customer complaints, are assessed and tracked through Customer surveys.

6.2 Business Planning

6.2.1 The product planning team, working with other resources (that is, marketing and sales), provides key data regarding the following subjects:

- Market analysis

- Competitive analysis

- Technology analysis

6.2.2 Business planning (annual strategic planning and annual operational planning) is the responsibility of the organization manager. That manager meets with the MSC and selected key individuals to evaluate the above listed inputs and to develop/ update the organization's annual strategic plan.

6.2.3 The MSC holds strategic plan review meetings annually (see example timetable in Figure 3A.2).

6.2.4 The strategic plan is the key output from this activity (see example plan contents in Figure 3A.3). The Escar product portfolio is included in the strategic plan. The Escar product portfolio is also published as a separate document and maintained by the product planning team throughout the year. The management system, process map, and processes are reviewed by the MSC and updated as appropriate.

6.2.5 The MSC translates strategic plan objectives for the upcoming year into specific financial and other action objectives for the operational balanced scorecard. Objectives are aligned with customer needs and expectations (requirements).

6.2.6 Balanced scorecard objectives are aligned with organization capability, and related metrics are tracked by the MSC.

6.2.7 Escar yearly operating plan sales objectives are aligned with marketing and sales capability and customer needs at the annual budget review meeting. Sales and marketing and corporate plans are adjusted to reduce the risk of poor product offering or new product introduction timing.

Section 6. Business Planning Procedure *(continued)*

6.2.8   The Escar MSC schedules specific new product projects and other initiatives needed to satisfy budget review and strategic plan objectives. Progress is tracked at monthly project review meetings, using selected metrics on the balanced scorecard.

6.2.9   Environmental and Health and Safety objectives will reflect risk analysis and legal and other requirements analysis for significance.

6.2.9   Changes needed in the management system, including the process map, will be included in the business plan.

6.3   Operations review process (balanced scorecard and monthly / quarterly / annual business review).

6.3.1   Formal operations review meetings are nominally held monthly (minimum of quarterly) with the MSC.

6.3.2   The operations review agenda includes items in 3A.1.

6.3.3   Metrics results are tracked against annual targets on the balanced scorecard and reviewed at the operations review meeting, along with specific support data. Improvement actions are identified and tracked. When indicated, the balanced scorecard is adjusted.

6.3.4   The annual operations review considers year-end operating plan, balanced scorecard, human resources, and other results data. Improvement recommendations are presented at the strategic planning meetings.

6.3.5   The operations review agenda items will cover the minimum requirements in Table 3A.1.

6.3.6   Operations review minutes include meeting output. This output includes the following:

- List of participants
- Action plans with assigned responsibilities and deadlines
- Decisions made on improving product, processes or the QMS, EMS, or OHSMS
- Revise / revising of missed targets
- Resource needs

6.4   Continuous Improvement

6.4.1   All Escar site organizations subscribe to and support the Escar continual improvement program practices.

6.4.2   Escar continual improvement program is the primary method used by the organizations for business process improvement, and the Escar continual improvement program criteria are used as a measurement tool.

6.4.3   An Escar continual improvement program self-assessment at the site level is conducted at least annually. Findings from this activity are integrated into annual planning.

Section 6. Business Planning Procedure *(continued)*

6.4.4 Organizations use the Plan, Do, Check, Act (PDCA) approach to improve business processes. Trend charts are also a tool that can be used to help manage for improvement. If needed, each organization site will establish cross-functional teams to address specific improvement opportunities.

6.4.5 All Organizations participate in the employee survey process. Human Resources conducts an annual survey. Data from the survey is analyzed and improvement actions are identified. The MSC shares survey results and planned improvement actions with employees at employee town hall meetings.

6.5 Planning deployment

6.5.1 To assure focused activity from all organization employees, the organization's vision and mission statements are communicated to employees using various means (for example: postings in the work area, and on websites and in presentations at employee town hall meetings and department staff meetings).

6.5.2 Pertinent Escar operational review meetings, continual improvement program actions, objectives/expectations, metrics, and the resulting BBS are communicated to employees using various means (see examples above).

6.5.3 Product development is aligned with Escar objectives; progress is tracked and reviewed by the Escar MSC at monthly project review meetings.

6.5.4 Personal performance is aligned with the Organization Balanced Scorecard And Results Tracked Quarterly (Evaluation Document or other tool). These performance results are included in the annual employee performance appraisal.

Table 3A.1 Operational review meeting minimum agenda requirements.
Note: Changes are included from Table 3.1 Management review topics matrix.
This company is not in the food industry and as such does not include FSMS topics.

1. Satisfaction feedback from customers, employees, suppliers, shareholders
2. Communication from all external parties on environmental and health and safety
3. Balanced scorecard objectives and results review (including quality, environmental and health/safety objectives)
4. Results of internal, external, and third-party audits/self assessments
5. Performance of processes (manufacturing and process map as applicable)
6. Environmental and Health/Safety performance (objectives)
7. Product conformity – internal PPM, scrap rate, customer complaints/returns
8. Status of incidents, corrective action and preventive action for QMS, EMS, and OHSMS
9. Follow-up actions from previous meetings
10. Changes to the business including the business management system impacts including QMS, EMS and OHSMS
11. Recommendations (opportunities) for improvement (required for balanced scorecard and operation review meeting metric presentations in each operation review meeting)
12. Cost of poor quality
13. Analysis of actual or potential field failures and their impact on quality, safety or the environment
14. Status of design projects
15. Delivered product quality performance (external ppm)
16. Customer disruptions (including field returns)
17. Delivery performance (including incidents requiring premium freight)
18. Notifications from customers on quality or delivery issues regarding supply status (such as, probation, etc.)
19. Review of all QMS requirements and performance trends (such as, annual internal audit opportunities for improvement tracking)
20. Results of consultation and participation
21. Review of systems updated (QMS, EMS, and OHSMS)

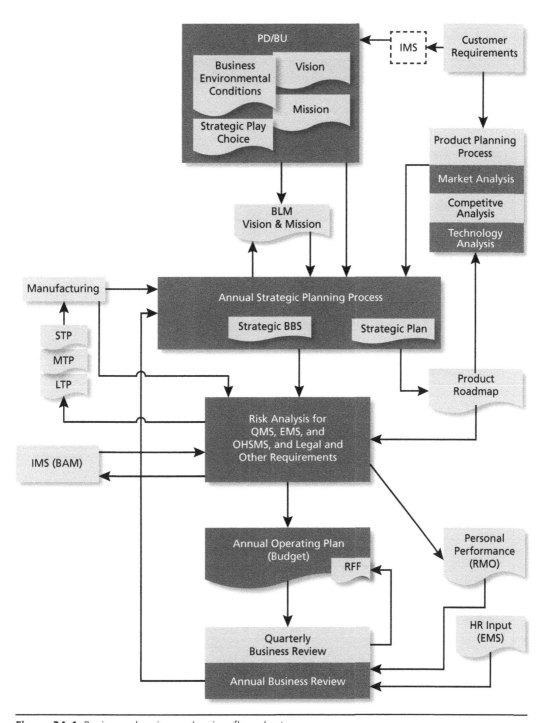

Figure 3A.1 Business planning and review flow chart.

Table 3A.2 Strategic plan timetable example.

Item	Due Date
Yearly Operating Budget (Finance)	Q3
Strategic Product Planning	Q3>Q4
Product and Marketing Strategy	1X1
Metric Goals (Current Year and 5-Year)	1X2
All Other Stakeholder Inputs/Updates	1X2
1st Draft Review	1X3
2nd Revision Updates	1X4
2nd Draft Review	2X1
Final Updates	2X2
Publish Final Document	2X2
Review by Organization Manager	2X3

Table 3A.3 Strategic plan table of contents example.

1. Vision/Mission
2. Executive Summary
3. Market Overview
4. Metrics
5. Product Strategy & Requirements
6. Logistics Requirements
7. Staffing
8. Financials
9. Plan Assembly and Administrative Support
10. Customer Expectations/Requirements and Customer Satisfaction
11. Business Management System Changes (including Process Map)

4

Integrated Risk Management and Enterprise Risk

Enterprise risk management is essential, especially to large global organizations. Simply said, without integrated and enterprise risk management, the General Manager of a site that has implemented QMS, EMS, OHSMS, and/or FSMS cannot answer this important question: What are the organization's highest risk areas in this site? Without integrated and enterprise risk management, the CEO of an organization cannot answer: What are the highest risk areas in the enterprise?

These are not trivial questions. Managing and mitigating risk is a key part of top management responsibility. Failure to understand and categorize risk in the enterprise often leads to little or no understanding of risk between the areas of Q, E, OHS, or FS in one site, let alone in the multiple sites of a large enterprise. Conducting risk evaluation consistently in order to understand, categorize, and control the organization's key risks is the topic addressed in this chapter.

QMS, EMS, OHSMS, and FSMS management systems require organizations to identify and control E, HS, and FS risks (for example, see Figure 4.1). When risk is evaluated for Q, E, OHS, or FS, we find that the same manufacturing process or high risk area is evaluated multiple times. Also, we find that in an enterprise, the Q, E, HS, or FS areas are rated again and again by different entities. Because different risk systems are used, the ratings vary wildly.

Consider aluminum wheels. Many aluminum wheel factories follow the same melting, casting, machining, and paint processes. Identical processes used in the same environmental context for humans, materials, and methods should have identical or similar risk numbers. How can we make this happen? That is the subject of this chapter. Without software, integrating risk and enterprise risk calculations will be close to impossible. Evaluating risk with software is the topic of Chapter 14.

USING THE SAME RISK METHODOLOGY PROCESS

In adopting risk management processes, it is important to understand that *risk* is always a function of *severity* times *occurrence* ($R = S \times O$). Severity should be evaluated as the highest risk event that can take place when a Q, E, HS, or FS failure takes place in the process or manufacturing area *without any controls* (that is, $S \times O$ where the occurrence is not adjusted by any controls). Residual risk is the amount of risk left over after current controls are applied. Current controls are the controls used by the organization to reduce occurrence and/or prevent or detect the failure. See Figure 4.2.

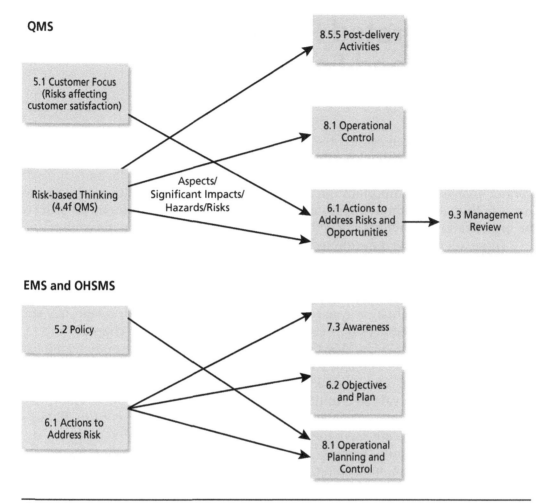

Figure 4.1 Managing risk in QMS, EMS, and OHS.

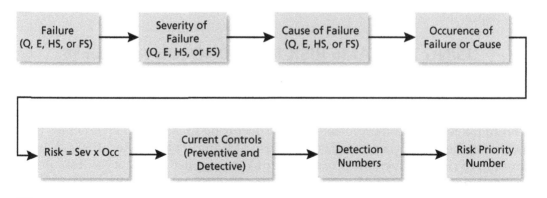

Figure 4.2 Current controls.

Any risk methodology tool that quantifies severity, occurrence, and residual risk can be used. All processes in the process map, including within the entire manufacturing plant, should be analyzed for risk. The analysis of risk in manufacturing can be conducted by one manufacturing department at a time and by one process in the department at a time. The failures for Q, E, HS, or FSMS should be analyzed for each process.

IDENTIFYING Q, E, AND HS RISK
IN A MANUFACTURING PROCESS

Consider this example. If a drilling operation creates a 5 mm round hole, the failure mode is oversize hole or undersize hole. Failure mode could also include chatter or burr in a hole if these could affect the characteristic requirement.

Next the process is analyzed to determine what failure in the drilling machine could cause environmental or health and safety issues. Here failure could include a negative environmental effect due to coolant leakage on the floor, a spill, or air borne coolant mist. Operator hazards (health and safety failures) include loose clothing caught in drilling equipment and chips flying off and causing injury. In this way Q, E, and HS failures are identified, and the highest severity event for each category is determined. (See sample column headings in Figure 4.3.)

Then the causes of each failure mode are identified. The occurrence (Occ) relates to the occurrence of the failure mode or the causes. The high severity (Sev) failure modes, those causing death or severe injury, and the highest risk events are determined. Preventive or detective controls that are employed in the site are identified and documented. Next a risk priority number (RPN) is calculated (Sev x Occ x Detection).

The environmental interaction of a process is called an "aspect" and it has an environmental "impact." Similarly, a process has a health and safety "hazard" which has a "severity." Depending on whether the risk assessment is for Q, E, HS, or FS, the terminology and the form column headings will change.

Table 1

Step			Requirement		Class	Potential Failure Modes	Potential Effects of Failure: Sev	Sev	Potential Causes of Failure	Preventive Controls	Occ	Sev* Occ	Detective Controls: Det	Det	RPN	Recommended Actions
ID	Description	Function	Product	Process												

Table 2

Step			Parameters		Deviation	Consequence: Sev	Sev	Causes	Safeguards	Occ	Sev* Occ	Detective Controls: Det	Det	RPN	Recommended Actions
ID	Description	Node	Type	Description											

Table 3

Step			Requirement		Hazards	Effects of Hazard: Sev	Sev	Causes of Hazards	Preventive Controls	Occ	Sev* Occ	Detective Controls: Det	Det	RPN	Recommended Actions
ID	Description	Function	Type	Description											

Table 4

Aspects					Potential Failure Mode	Impacts of Aspect: Sev	Sev	Causes of Aspect	Preventive Controls	Occ	Detective Controls: Det	Det	RPN	Recommended Actions
Step ID	Step Description	Function	Description	Type										

Table 5

Step		Requirement		Potential Hazards	Potential Causes	Preventive Controls	Occ	Potential Effects: Sev	Sev	Sev* Occ	Signf?	CCP / OPRP / CQP	Reason for Decision	Detective Controls: Det	Det	RPN
ID	Description	ID	Description													

Figure 4.3 Sample column headings for risk assessment.

IDENTIFYING Q, E, AND HS RISK IN THE PROCESS MAP

For example, one could calculate the Q, E, and HS risks in a purchasing process. The Q risk can be calculated by identifying the requirements of the purchasing process (qualified suppliers, high value products, on-time delivery). Failures for quality are then identified: unqualified suppliers, poor quality products, and late delivery. Subsequently, the severity, cause, and controls for these failures will be identified including severity, occurrence, and detection numbers.

Environmental risks could be that the "purchased goods cause environmental damage to the planet (for example, excessive or non-recyclable dunnage) or purchased good causes environmental damage in the product (if it is assembled into the product)."

An example of health and safety risk could be that the "purchased product causes health or safety hazards to the personnel in the plant" (for example, due to generating excessive dust or including allergens). In the case of a service being performed, it could be "purchased product is performed in a manner that the service personnel injure themselves."

In this manner, each process in the process map, including manufacturing, is analyzed for risk using the same process allowing the plant and the enterprise to compare numbers calculated by the risk. However, we need to do a little more work, as explained in the next section, to compare risk numbers.

UNDERSTANDING SEVERITY, OCCURRENCE, AND DETECTION

Severity is a relative measure of the effect of any action that can occur in an organization. Severity does not consider the probability of occurrence of the event. If it is possible that an event can occur, severity indicates its impact to the organization, users, and employees when it does occur. Failures with the potential for high severity should be a concern to top management.

The next level of importance includes those items with a potential for high risk (that is, high severity times occurrence). These items should be a focus of the organization to ensure that controls are indeed in place. Lastly, the RPN is the amount of risk remaining in the organization after the controls are in place. They represent the residual risk to the organization (that is, after the controls are in place).

SEVERITY, OCCURRENCE, AND DETECTION RATINGS

Severity, occurrence, and detection ratings are assigned via tables typically rated from 1 through 10. A rating of 10 represents the worst severity and 1 the least. Similarly for occurrence and detection, 10 is the worst number and 1 is the best in the context of risk management. In order for risk numbers to be comparable between Q, E, HS, and FS, the ratings have to be comparable.

Some approaches, independently applied, use scales that go from 1 to 4 or 5. It's interesting to note that interpretations of highest and lowest ratings are usually readily agreed upon regardless of the scale. Disagreements arise about the in-between numbers relative to Q, E, HS, or FS. However, to be able to compare risks between the different standards, the relative ratings need to be the same. Tables 4.1, 4.2, and 4.3 provide an example of commonly used ratings. These tables do not have to be used as is. We typically adjust the tables to fit the organization or industry and use different tables for automotive, aerospace, service, or food.

Table 4.1 Severity table standardization.

Rank	QMS		EMS	OHSMS
	Product	Process		
10	Affects safe product operation and/or involves noncompliance with government regulation without warning.	May endanger operator (machine or assembly) without warning	Extensive detrimental long term impact, chronic release of persistent hazardous pollutant	Multiple fatal effects on human health
9	Affects safe product operation and/or regulatory requiren	May endanger operator		Catastrophic
8	Major Disruptic			
7	Significa Disruptic			
6	Moderat Disruptic			
5	Moderat Disruptic			
4				
3	Moderat Disruptic			
2	Minor Disruption			Appearance operable, iter noticed by di
1	No Effect			No discernibl

Table 4.2 Occurrence table standardization.

Rank	QMS	EMS	OHSMS
10	Persistent Failures	≥ 1 in 10	Has occurred previously and will probably occur again (80-100% chance); (for example, once every month)	Frequent	Has occurred previously and will probab (80-100% chance); (for example, once e
9			Frequent	ously and is likely to c (for example, every 1
8	Freque Failure			n the past; possibility 0% chance); (for exam
7				n the past; a small cha (2-20% chance); (for
6	Occassic Failur			
5				I in the past and is un ance)
4	Realtiv Few Fail			
3				convenience or ns
2	Failure Unlike			rnable effect
1				

Table 4.3 Standardization of detection tables.

Rank	Likelihood of Detection	QMS	EMS	OHSMS
10	Absolute Uncertainty	No detection opportunity		
9	Very Remote	Not likely to detect; for example, Random Audits		
8	Remote	Defect Detection Post Processing (qualitative measurement)		
7	Very Low	Defect Detection at Source (qualitative measurement)		
6	Low	Defect Detection Post Processing (quantitative measurement)		
5	Moderate	Defect Detection at Source (quantitative measurement)		
4	Moderately high	Mistake Proofing Post Processing		
3	High	Mistake Proofing at Source		

FMEA AND HACCP METHODOLOGIES

Created by the NASA space program, FMEA (Failure Mode and Effects Analysis) and HACCP (Hazard Analysis and Critical Control Points) have the same historical origin. FMEA methodology was used to predict both design and process failures and was picked up by many industries including aerospace. FMEA became a much sought after tool after the US and then the European automotive industry used it as a preventive tool to improve quality from percent defectives to less than 30 ppm. Though many different tools deserve credit—including advance quality planning, disciplined problem solving, and error proofing—FMEA is widely acknowledged as being a very important tool in the arsenal for prevention.

FMEA

During the 1980s, much work was done with the process FMEA and the control plan. The authors wrote an important methodology called Process Review. This links process flow, PFMEA, and control plans to drive improvement when implementing a Ford program called Q 101. At the same time, Gregory Gruska helped Ford Powertrain with a methodology called Dimensional Control Plans (now known as Dynamic Control Plans). Credit also goes to the Ford, GM, and Chrysler teams working under the auspices of AIAG in writing an FMEA standard guideline in the 1990s. Omnex's Kevin Lange was a member of one of the initial writing committees and Greg Gruska is currently on the writing committee for the FMEA. In the early 2000s, the authors began using FMEAs and standardized risk methodologies for environmental and health and safety risks, publishing papers on integrated management systems. In the 2010 time frame, the authors integrated HACCP and FMEA methodologies as shown later in this chapter.

HACCP

HACCP (pronounced has'sip) originated when NASA asked Pillsbury whether they could provide food with zero risk to the astronauts in the space program. HACCP not only includes the examination of the risk of food preparation, but also includes control points to mitigate the risk.

> A **hazard** is an effect of a failure mode (malfunction) that results in injury to a human.

Because food safety deals with protecting humans from injury, risk analysis typically uses the HACCP approach. HACCP methodology uses a HACCP plan that identifies critical control points and methods to control the (causes of) hazards. Similarly, FMEA methodology uses control plans to identify methods to control the (causes of) failure modes. The basic HACCP process only examines the critical controls, whereas the FMEA process looks at controlling all characteristics, not only critical points.

In HACCP, critical controls are identified by following the chart shown in Figure 4.4 from the Codex Alimentarius Commission created by the UN in 1963.

The authors created FMEA-inspired forms for HACCP that can be used to integrate Q, E, HS, and FS risks (Figure 4.5).

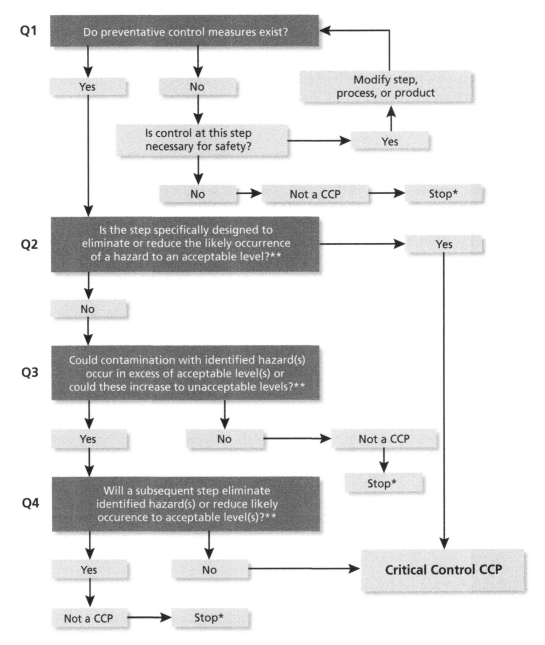

* *Proceed to the next identified hazard in the described process*
** *Acceptable and unacceptable levels need to be determined within the overall objectives in identifying the CCPs of the HACCP plan*

Figure 4.4 HACCP critical controls chart.

(HAACP Analysis Worksheet)

Monterey Jack for Commercial Sales

Item: Cheese Production   Process Responsibility: D Adeina   HACCP: 848NY   Prepared By: J. Kathleen

Description: Monterey Jack with and without additives   Date (Orig.): 11/10/2014 (Rev.) 2

Core Team: Cheese Production Team #1

Step		Requirement		Potential Hazards	Potential Causes	Preventive Controls	Occ	Potential Effects: Sev	Sev	Sev/Occ	Signf?	CCP/OPRP/CQP	Reason for Decision	Detective Controls: Det	Det	RPN
ID	Description	ID	Description													
10	Receiving											OPRP				
20	Inspection															
30	Standardize Milk											CQP				
40	Bulk Storage															
50	Pasteurize Milk	@H001	No Biological Hazards	Campylobacteriosis	Wrong settings	Setup Min Temp Setup Min Time	2	Infection:10	10	20	Y	CCP/CQP	Bacteria on cattle can contaminate the milk on these animals (cowshare)	EOL Batch Sampling:6	6	120
				E-Coli O157 H7	Wrong settings	Setup Min Temp Setup Min Time	2	Toxin-mediated Infection:10	10	20	Y		Bacteria found in raw milk	EOL Batch Sampling:6	6	120
				Listeriosis	Wrong settings	Setup Min Temp Setup Min Time	2	Infection:10	10	20	Y		Bacteria found in unpasturized milk	EOL Batch Sampling:6	6	120
				Salmonellosis	Wrong settings	Setup Min Temp Setup Min Time	2	Infection:10	10	20	Y		Bacteria found in raw milk	EOL Batch Sampling:6	6	120
				Shigellosis	Wrong settings	Setup Min Temp Setup Min Time	2	Toxin-mediated infection:10	10	20	Y		Bacteria found in milk;organisms multiply at room temperature	EOL Batch Sampling:6	6	120

HACCP Plan Worksheet

Monterey Jack for Commercial Sales

HACCP Number: SQF-845   Date (Orig.): 11/17/2014   Date (Rev.): 11/17/2014

Product ID: MJ-138947   Company: Key Contact: Dalia Adena   Phone: 555-1234

Product Name: Cheese Production   Address: EMail:

Description: Monterey Jack with and without additives   City, State Zip:

Step		Requirements		Control Method	Critical Limits	Monitoring	Sample Size	Frequency	Corrective Action	Verification	Records
ID	Description	ID	Description								
OPRP 10	Receiving										
CQP 30	Standardize Milk										
	20	Inspection									
	40	Bulk Storage									
CCP/CQP 50	Pasteurize Milk	@H001	No Biological Hazards	EOL Batch Sampling							
				Setup Min Temp	C 161 F	continuous computer monitoring	100%		computer controlled diverter valve	Part of layered audits	raw data and summary reports by control program
				Setup Min Time	C 15 sec at temp	continuous computer monitoring	100%		computer controlled diverter valve	Part of layered audits	raw data and summary reports by control program
		@H002	No Chemical Hazards	(Prerequisite Process Control)							
				PRP: Supplier Mgt	C Supplier management criteria	Supplier management monitoring program	100%		remove from acceptable supplier list	Part of layered audits	audit checklists

Figure 4.5 FMEA-inspired HACCP sheets.

ENTERPRISE RISK

Organizations with multiple sites often have several locations that make similar products using similar manufacturing processes (see Figure 4.6). This drives enterprise risk. Simply stated, products and processes can be grouped into product and process families. These product families can be a "gear" family or a "baked good" family. The manufacturing processes in a gear family are often the same or similar and it is the same with the baked good family. The "parent" (primary product/process template) in a family may be in one site, but the "children" may be scattered all over the globe. Evaluating Q, E, HS, and FS risks is time consuming and costly. When risk is evaluated with the family concept in mind, risks can cascade to the children in a family from the parent.

Evaluation of enterprise risk then fundamentally saves time and money. When this evaluation is conducted in concert with the introduction of a new product or process, it is possible to take lessons learned into the new products and processes for Q, E, HS, and FS risks. Furthermore, when the risks are calculated using the same risk methodology and standardized tables, then the risk numbers can be compared between sites in an enterprise.

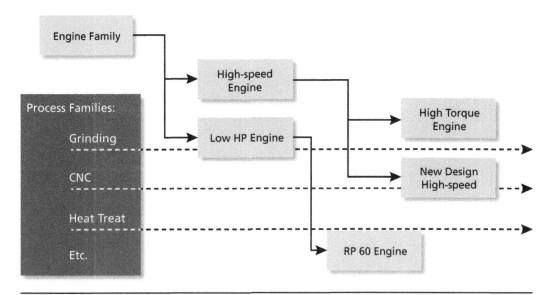

Figure 4.6 Enterprise risk example.
Note: Products inherit from the family. Processes cut across families.

The CEO is able to answer the questions about, a) the highest risk site of the organization and, b) the organization's highest risk products, processes, or events. As mentioned earlier, the highest risk and severity events need to be tested to ensure they are working. Enterprise risk analysis will help take us in this much needed direction. Of course, having risk software will also aid companies seeking to implement integrated and enterprise risk analysis, a topic of Chapter 12.

5

Conducting Integrated Audits

Integrated audits can only be performed in an organization with an integrated management system. However, integrating the internal audits is usually one of the first thing companies want to do in relationship to integration. Integrated audits allow for fewer days of audits for both internal and external audits and hence reduce costs. Even though the total time goes down by 20%, due to the reduction of the number of processes (in our example from Chapter 1) in one site from 300 to 100, each process actually get close to 200% of additional audit time. Reduced costs and more auditing time for the integrated processes, what is there not to love about integrated audits?

INTEGRATED AUDITS

Integrated audits at a minimum means one audit process, an integrated audit schedule, integrated forms including checklists, and a team capable of conducting an integrated audit. In a system that is not integrated there are typically three different internal audit processes and process owners. In an integrated audit, there is one audit process with one process owner. The audit process has one audit schedule instead of three different schedules. See Table 5.1. Properly executed audits need to capture the information required by ISO 19011. Some of the audit forms that capture this information include—opening and closing meeting attendees, audit plan, non-conformance forms, and audit report format (see Figure 5.2).

Table 5.1 Integrated audit schedule.

2015 Audit Schedule					
January I: 1/15-1/18 C: 1/22	February PR: 2/12	March P: 3/10	April PR: 4/15	May P: 5/12	June PR: 6/15
July I: 7/12-7/15 C: 7/22	August PR: 8/12	September P: 9/11	October PR: 10/12	November P: 11/12	December PR: 12/12
Legend: I = IMS Audit C = Compliance to EHS P = Process Audits PR = Product Audits					

Integrated audit checklists (see Table 5.2) integrate the requirements of QMS, EMS, OHSMS, and, if required, FSMS. Book two on integrated management systems, that is, on integrated audits, will provide an integrated audit checklist. This book's recommendation is to write the requirements around the process and an open-ended checklist such as shown in Figure 5.1. In this way, the auditors do not need to study the standard, but can study their organization's own processes. However, auditors will need to create an integrated audit plan, sample the different areas including Q, E, HS, or FS and document the evidence in their audit checklists and learn many competencies focused on conducting an integrated audit. In fact, integrated audit teams are the next topic in regards to integrated audits.

What should be the characteristics of an integrated audit team? First, the audit team needs to be made up of top management personnel, and quality, environmental, health/safety, and food safety experts based on the different areas that need to be audited. There are many processes focused on top management such as policy, objective setting, continual improvement, and management review that can be performed by the top management representative on the team. The remaining processes can be distributed among the other experts on the team. The different audit trails of an integrated audit are shown in Figures 5.3-5.6, illustrating how an audit can be distributed among the different constituents in an integrated audit. The audit can be conducted by two audit teams each representing Q, E, HS, or FS. Team members can double team during this audit if needed. Especially, the audit requires expertise in the respective audit areas of Q, E, HS, or FS (especially HACCP). In time, all auditors will become proficient in all areas if they audit together long enough. Integrated audit competencies include—audit planning, sampling integrated audits, interviewing integrated areas to ensure coverage of Q, E, HS, and FS criteria, writing integrated audit nonconformances, and then sampling for the close out phase of the audit.

OMNEX
325 E. Eisenhower, Suite 4
Ann Arbor, MI 48108

Organization: __XYZ Aluminum Wheels__ Date: __February 12, 2015__

Auditor(s) Name: __Jim Cook(JC)/ Chad Kymal (CK)__

INTEGRATED MANAGEMENT SYSTEMS AUDIT PLAN
(ISO 9001, ISO 14001, AND OHSAS 18001)

Date	Time	Activity	Person(s) Interviewed
Feb 12	8:00 – 8:30	Opening Meeting	
	8:30 – 9:30	Plant Tour	
	9:30 – 10:00	Business Review (JC); Recruiting, Training (CK)	
	10:00 – 11:00	Strategic Planning (JC); Recruiting, Training (CK)	
	11:00 – 12:00	Customer Complaints (JC); Training & Motivation (CK)	
	12:00 – 1:00	Lunch/Auditor Meeting	

Corrective Action Request				
Part A	**Audit Information**			
Department	Molding	**Audit Number**	101	
Activity Audited	Operator Training	**Car Number**	DAO-05	
Auditor	Bob Roberts	**Date Issued**	11/17	
Reference	ISO 9001, ISO 14001 and OHSAS 18001			
Part B	**Nonconformity**			

Nonconformity: The document control process is not effective.

Requirement: Clause 4.2.3.d. ISO 9001: 2008; Clause 4.4.5.d. ISO 14001: 2004; Clause 4.4.5.d. OHSAS 18001: 2007 "....*ensure that relevant versions of applicable documents are available at points of use....*"

Objective Evidence: Operator Instruction for the Molding Machine Number 50 in the molding area showing revision level C and the Master list shows the current revision level as D a few months ago.

Auditor	Date	Department Representative	Date

Figure 5.1 Audit form example (Omnex).

ABC CORP
Taipei Office, Taiwan (4 days)

ISO/TS 16949:2009 and ISO 14001:2004
April 13, 2014 to April 17, 2014
Final Report

Lead Auditor: Chad Kymal and G. Gruska
Client Contact: Dave Young and Mike Childs

Index

Client information

Company Name: ABC Corp   **Tel: 886-2-xxxx-xxxx**

Contact Name: Dave Young   **Fax: 886-2-xxxx-xxxx**

Department/Processes: All Processes; Refer to Process Map in Policy Manual
(Note: In Taipei Office the main processes are Sales, Marketing, Software Development and FAE)

Address: No name Street, Taipei City 105, Taiwan

- Scope of Audit: ISO/TS 16949:2009 Except for 7.5.1.3, 7.5.1.5, 7.5.1.8, 7.5.2, 7.5.4.1, 8.2.3.1 and 8.2.4 and ISO 14001:2004

- Product – All products except some products under waiver including E commerce

Dates of Audit: 04/13/2014 to 04/17/2014

Locations: ABC Corp, Taipei, Taiwan

Type of Audit:

☐ QM or Doc. Review   ☐ Gap   ☒ Internal   ☒ System   ☐ Sweep Audit   ☐ Process

Lead Auditor Signature: Chad Kymal

(The remaining pages of the audit report were not included)

Figure 5.2 Audit form example (ABC Corp).

INTEGRATED AUDIT TYPES

Integrated audit types include system audits, manufacturing process audits, layered process audits, product audits, and compliance audits:

- A system audit is a snapshot in time of the effectiveness of an entire system. A system audit will cover all processes and all clauses of each of the standards in the integrated management system (Q, E, H, or FS).

- Manufacturing process audits ensure that manufacturing processes are performing as planned and per the controls for Q, E, HS, and FS. It ensures that work instructions and other manufacturing process requirements are being fulfilled.

- Layered process audits are random audits performed by various levels of management (from top management to supervisors) who randomly visit processes to ensure specific controls are being followed by the operator. Layered process audits are similar to manufacturing process audits; the goal is not just to check the controls, but to show management's interest and commitment and the importance of the audit for operational controls (Q, E, HS, and FS).

- Product audits ensure that product inspections required by the organization are followed. Dock audits fall into the category of product audits. Dock audits ensure that the company's packaging requirements are followed (Q, E, HS, and FS).

- Compliance audits comprehensively evaluate the organization's compliance to legal and state requirements to Q, E, HS, and FS requirements.

Table 5.2 Integrated audit checklist for the training process.

Integrated ISO 9001-ISO 14001-ISO 45001-FSSC 2200 Audit Checklist – Competence, Training, and Awareness					
Doc. #	Requirements	What to Audit	Notes & Objective Evidence	Stage I (Y/N)	Stage II (Y/N)
ISO 9001 ISO 14001 ISO 45001	Competence				
	The organization shall a) determine the necessary competence of person(s) doing work under its control that affects its quality performance; environmental performance, and OH&S Performance;	Are there competency requirements defined for different types of positions? (Make sure all types of employees are sampled from Top Management, Middle management, Engineers, and Operators) Who affects Quality – Everyone; who affects Environmental and OH&S Performance, everyone for awareness, but especially those that are shown to affect Environmental and OH&S as per the risk assessments.			
	b) ensure that these persons are competent on the basis of appropriate education, training, or experience;	Are their records that show the competency based on education, training or experience? Note, on the job training is also considered training.			
	c) where applicable, take actions to acquire the necessary competence, and evaluate the effectiveness of the actions taken;	Are there are actions taken when personnel are not found competent and are employees reevaluated to ensure effectiveness of actions taken. For OH&S see guidance below.			
	d) retain appropriate documented information as evidence of competence. NOTE Applicable actions can include, for example, the provision of training to, the mentoring of, or the reassignment of currently employed persons; or the hiring or contracting of competent persons. (ISO 9001, ISO 14001 and ISO 45001)				

(Continued)

Table 5.2 Integrated audit checklist for the training process.   *(Continued)*

Integrated ISO 9001-ISO 14001-ISO 45001-FSSC 2200 Audit Checklist – Competence, Training, and Awareness					
Doc. #	Requirements	What to Audit	Notes & Objective Evidence	Stage I (Y/N)	Stage II (Y/N)
ISO 9001 ISO 14001 ISO 45001	Competence				
	ISO 45001 (only): Actions taken to ensure competence, including training, shall take into account: • the hazards identified and associated risks assessed by the organization; • preventive and control measures resulting from the risk assessment process; • assigned roles and responsibilities; • individual capabilities, including language skills and literacy; • the relevant updating of the competencies if necessary (context or work changes). NOTE 1: Necessary competencies also include those prescribed by regulation. NOTE 2: Applicable actions can include, for example, the provision of training to, the mentoring of, or the re-assignment of currently employed persons; or the hiring or contracting of competent persons. NOTE 3: Workers and worker representatives can assist in both identifying needs and assisting in building necessary competencies.				
		Is there a training plan to satisfy these needs? Is it followed? **Objective Evidence:** Training plan			

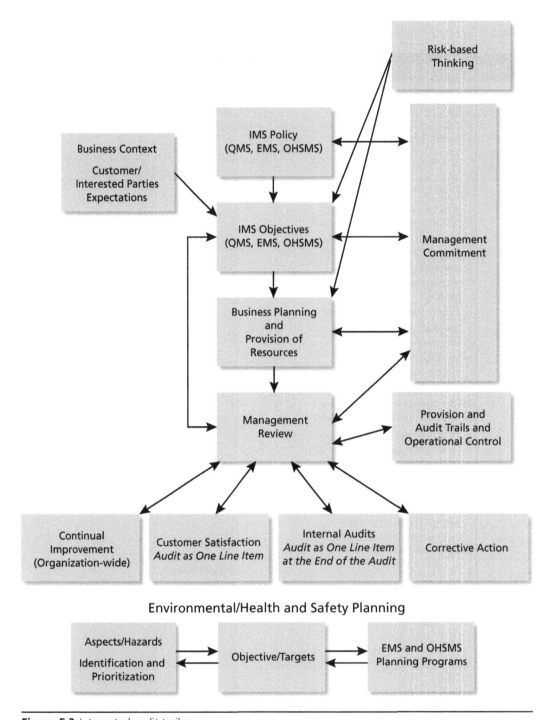

Figure 5.3 Integrated audit trails.

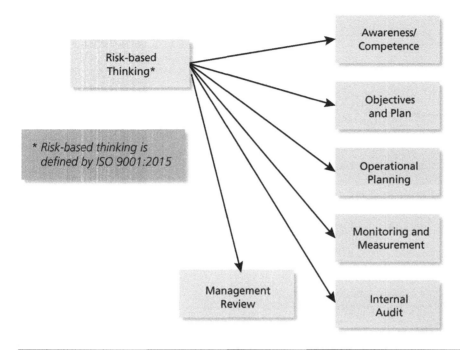

Figure 5.4 Risk audit trail.

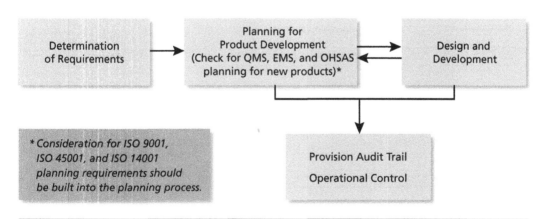

Figure 5.5 New product realization audit trail.

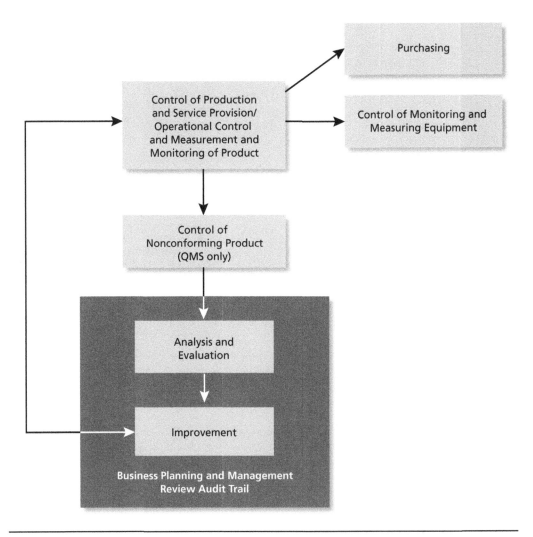

Figure 5.6 Provision audit trail.

Integrated Audit Competencies

1. **Describe the relationship between the clauses of the different standards.**
   It's not necessary that everyone on the audit team have this competency. However, the best auditors will know each of the standards being considered for the IMS (and their clauses), whether it is QMS, EMS, OHSMS, or FSMS.

2. **List the requirements of the clauses and the difference between the comparable clauses.**
   This competency goes hand in hand with the one above. It's necessary to understand not only the standards and the requirements. It's also necessary to understand, to the detailed level of the "shalls," the requirements in the comparable clauses. What is different and what is unique to each of the Q, E, HS, and FS standards?

3. **Conduct document review to the Q, E, HS, and FS standards.**
   Only the lead auditor on the team needs to have this competency. The IMS lead auditor should know the documentation requirements of each of the standards and be able to evaluate each procedure against the "shalls" of the respective standards, whether it is Q, E, HS, or FS.

4. **Create IMS audit plans and prioritize the audit.**
   The IMS lead auditor should be able to analyze the performance data of the Q, E, HS, and FS management systems, prioritize the audit, and create a process oriented checklist.

5. **Conduct opening and closing meetings for integrated management systems.**
   The opening and closing meetings for different management system standards are essentially the same, but there are a few differences between some of the standards.

6. **Interview process owners and audit integrated processes.**
   All auditors on the audit team should be able to interview the process owners and audit the processes. It would be best if all the auditors had the knowledge of competencies 1 and 2 on this list. However, customized checklists with instructions on sampling made especially for the organization's processes could eliminate the need to retain knowledge of all the standards and their requirements. Another competency that goes hand in hand with auditing an integrated process is the ability to sample the different streams of Q, E, HS, and FS.

7. **Write non conformances for integrated management systems.**
   Each auditor on the audit team should be able to write non-conformances for integrated processes

8. **Conduct close outs for integrated management systems.**
   Close outs require that the auditor determine whether the organization implemented all the actions taken in the close out whether actions were effective. One of the competencies required is the ability to sample an integrated process for close out.

ENTERPRISE AUDITS

Although it is difficult to implement integrated audits in one site, it is even more difficult to implement them across the enterprise. In an enterprise, similar to the site rules for integration, there can be only one audit process, one integrated audit schedule (sorted by sites), and integrated forms including checklists across the enterprise. The team conducting the internal audits can be the same team across the enterprise for audit consistency or different teams in each site. There are pros and cons for both choices in this decision. In the end, it comes down to cost and the need for audit effectiveness. An enterprise needs additional guidelines for consistency. In this section we will focus on auditing effectiveness rules for an enterprise audit.

Audit Program

The enterprise procedure should clearly specify what audit programs are allowed in the enterprise in the scope of the procedure. For example, an enterprise could be integrating ISO 9001, ISO 14001, and ISO 45001. If a site has not fully integrated, what is the deadline for integration? Does the enterprise allow any site not to integrate any of the management systems? All audit programs including Housekeeping, Safety, 5S (lean manufacturing), and ISO 17025 (lab management systems) should be included in the audit program section. Of course, the scope statement of the procedure should specify which programs are included in the enterprise audit procedure.

Audit Programs and Audit Types

Each audit program can include specific audit types. For the integrated audit, audit types could include system audits, manufacturing process audits, layered process audits, product audits, and compliance audits. A description of each of the audit types is provided earlier in this chapter.

Forms/Checklists

For each audit type, it's necessary to standardize forms in the enterprise. Forms to be standardized include audit plan, nonconformance, opening and closing meeting agendas and attendee list, process to clause matrix, and others. Standardization should include an audit report format. Audit report formats are standardized in automotive, aerospace, and other industries. Organizations can use the Omnex audit report format (Figure 5.1) or formats used by the automotive and aerospace industries. The relationship of audit programs to audit types to audit forms is shown in Figure 5.7.

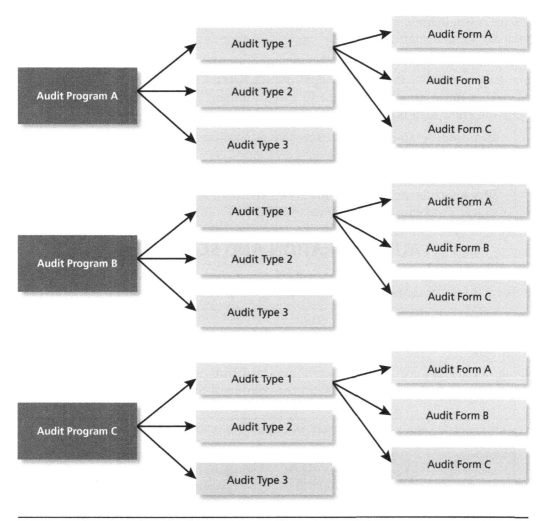

Figure 5.7 The relationship of audit programs to audit types to audit forms.

CORRECTIVE ACTION CATEGORIES

Typically, organizations use categories including *major, minor,* and *opportunity for improvement.* Sometimes, organizations add a category called *critical* that supersedes a major nonconformance. Here is a description of each category.

Critical: A failure that could cause the death of someone in the site or external to the site.

Major: A breakdown of a process or a missing process or clause; a number of minor issues resulting in a breakdown; a product with quality or food safety issues that could be shipped to the customer; an environmental or health and safety issue that could cause harm to someone working in the site; non-compliance with a regulation that can result in a large fine.

Minor: A single incident or failure in quality, environmental, health/safety, or food safety of a minor nature.

Opportunity for improvement: An improvement opportunity that is present in the plant. It cannot be incident specific, which would make it a recommendation. Also, it is not a nonconformance to a requirement in the standard. If there is a nonconformance, it is either a critical, major, or minor nonconformance.

> Example: Scrap in plant is excessive as compared to similar production in Plant XYZ. – OFI.

> Example: Conduct 8D problem solving for oversize ID on part 123. (Because it is incident specific and is telling the organization what to do, this is a recommendation, not an OFI.)

AUDIT DURATION AND SCHEDULE

Enterprise audits can standardize audit duration for each audit type by stipulating either a minimum time or a duration using existing standard tables. For example:

> "Use QMS, EMS, OHSMS, and FSMS tables listed below. For duration for system audits, add the total time and do not go below 50% of the combined time."

Table 5.3 and 5.4 are used by each standard individually. Integrated audits by third-party registrars will use 20% of the combined time.

Table 5.3 Audit duration by standard: QMS, EMS, OHSMS, and FSMS (ISO 22000 and FSSC 22000).*

# of Employees	Audit Days				# of Employees	Audit Days			
	High	Med	Low	Lim.		High	Med	Low	Lim.
1 – 5	3.0	2.5	2.5	2.5	626 – 875	17.0	13.0	10.0	6.5
6 – 10	3.5	3.0	3.0	3.0	876 – 1175	19.0	15.0	11.0	7.0
11 – 15	4.5	3.5	3	3	1176 – 1550	20.0	16.0	12.0	7.5
16 – 25	5.5	4.5	3.5	3.0	1551 – 2025	21.0	17.0	12.0	8.0
26 – 45	7.0	5.5	4.0	3.0	2026 – 2675	23.0	18.0	13.0	8.5
46 – 65	8.0	6.0	4.5	3.5	2676 – 3450	25.0	19.0	14.0	9.0
66 – 85	9.0	7.0	5.0	3.5	3451 – 4350	27.0	20.0	15.0	10.0
86 – 125	11.0	8.0	5.5	4.0	4351 – 5450	28.0	21.0	16.0	11.0
126 – 175	12.0	9.0	6.0	4.5	5451 – 6800	30.0	23.0	17.0	12.0
176 – 275	13.0	10.0	7.0	5.0	6801 – 8500	32.0	25.0	19.0	13.0
276 – 425	15.0	11.0	8.0	5.5	8501 – 10700	34.0	27.0	20.0	14.0
426 – 625	16.0	12.0	9.0	6.0	> 10700	Follow progression above			

* Note: Audit days estimates may change after the new ISO 9001, 14001, and ISO 45001 are issued.

Table 5.4 Audit duration for FSSC 22000.*

Category	D Basic On-site Audit Time (in audit days)	H For Each Additional HACCP Study (in audit days)	MS Absence of Certified Relevant Management System (in audit days)	FTE # of Employees (in audit days)	For Each Additional Site Visited
A. Farming 1 (animals)	.75	.25			
B. Farming 2 (plants)	.75	.25			
C. Processing 1 (perishable animal products)	1.5	.50			
D. Processing 2 (perishable vegetal products)	1.0	.50		1 to 19 = 0 20 to 49 = 0.5 50 to 79 = 1.0	
E. Processing 3 (products with shelf life at ambient temperature)	1.5	.50		80 to 199 = 1.5 200 to 499 = 2.0	
F. Feed Production	1.5	.50	0.25	500 to 899 = 2.5 900 to 1,299 = 3.0	50% of minimum on-site audit time
G. Catering	1.0	.50		1,300 to 1,699 = 3.5	
H. Distribution	1.0	.50		1,700 to 2,999 = 4.0	
I. Services	1.0	.25		3,000 to 5,000 = 4.5	
J. Transport and Storage	1.0	.25		More than 5,000 = 5.0	
K. Equipment Manufacturing	1.0	.25			
L. (Bio)chemical Manufacturing	1.5	.50			
M. Packaging Material Manufacturing	1.0	.25			

* Note: Audit days estimates may change after the updated ISO 22000 is issued.

AUDITOR QUALIFICATION

This is another area that should be standardized in an enterprise audit. What should be the number of years of experience and educational backgrounds of the potential auditors? Should they have taken an internal auditor course or a lead auditor course? How many audits should they participate in before they are allowed to audit? Will there be a witness audit? What criteria will the witness audit use for certifying an auditor?

As we mentioned earlier, it is good to have at least one auditor on the audit team who is a member of top management. Others can have a Q, E, HS, or FS proficiency. At a minimum, auditors should have a high school diploma and five years of work experience. Auditors with college degrees can have a minimum of three years of experience. It is best if the organization has a few auditors who have passed a lead auditor class. All of the other auditors could be internal auditor certified. It is best if all the auditors are trained in the same course or by the same provider, since this could be a foundation source of variation that could cause much difficulty between sites and auditors.

Auditors should participate and be double teamed in at least two audits and then witnessed before they conduct an audit. A mixture ISO 19011 and the organization's requirements for internal audits can be the criteria used for the witness audit.

PERFORMANCE ANALYSIS AND CONTINUAL IMPROVEMENT

It is important that the enterprise have standardized performance measures. A few of the performance measures include a trend chart of the number of non-conformances (NCs) per site by audit type, and Pareto analysis showing which process, department, or clause had the highest number of NCs. See Figures 5.8 and 5.9. Other performance measures include a comparison of NCs between sites and also a comparison of the top Pareto items (see Figure 5.10).

The NCs should be compared to what the external auditors are finding. Differences in what is being found by the third party and internal audits can indicate opportunities for improvement.

Randomly, two or three corporate audits could be performed by known auditors to ensure the quality of the site internal audits. Also, yearly witness audits should be done to check on the quality of the internal auditors.

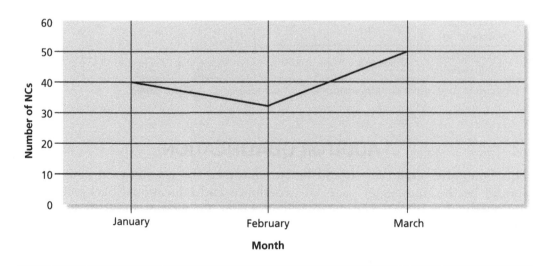

Figure 5.8 Trend chart of nonconformance by month.

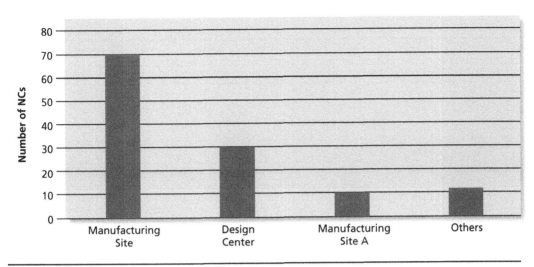

Figure 5.9 Pareto analysis of nonconformances between sites.

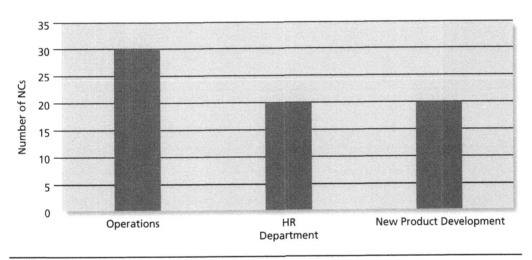

Figure 5.10 Pareto analysis of departments within Site C.

6

How An Integrated and Standardized Management System Performs for Maximum Effectiveness

An integrated enterprise is a model of efficiency with streamlined and standardized processes. Global and local process owners and processes are measured and perform processes in uniform fashion globally. In order to achieve its maximum effectiveness, the implementation would need to be assisted with web based work flows with what we will call an enterprise wide integrated management system to help accomplish what is described in this chapter. Furthermore, the implementation will need to follow and use the principles defined in the Business Planning, New Product Development, and Manufacturing Processes sections as described in this chapter. Properly implemented, an integrated enterprise has a competitive advantage over any rival in their business segment. Why? How? Let us discover it in this chapter.

PROCESS MAPS AND PROCESS DEFINITIONS

Organizations will benefit from redesigning processes when an integrated management system is contemplated. The first order of business is to identify enterprise and site processes. Flows originating from corporate management to the entire organization are categorized as enterprise flows.

Enterprise Processes

Enterprise processes are the flows that originate with and are coordinated by corporate. Enterprise processes flow between corporate and sites:

- Policy, Objectives, Business Plan and Reviews (Performance Management)
- Sales and Contract Review
- New Product Introduction
- Scheduling to Delivery
- Training, Competency, and Benefits
- Direct Purchasing
- Customer Satisfaction
- Continual Improvement Programs (Performance Management)
- Internal Audits

Site Processes

Site processes are flows that are site-specific, such as:

- Manufacturing
- Receiving
- Shipping
- Corrective Action
- Preventive Action
- Risk and Change Management
- Calibration and MSA
- Nonconforming Product
- Indirect purchasing
- Document and Records Control

Note: All processes highlighted are covered in this chapter.

Figure 6.1 shows how the enterprise processes and site processes interact.

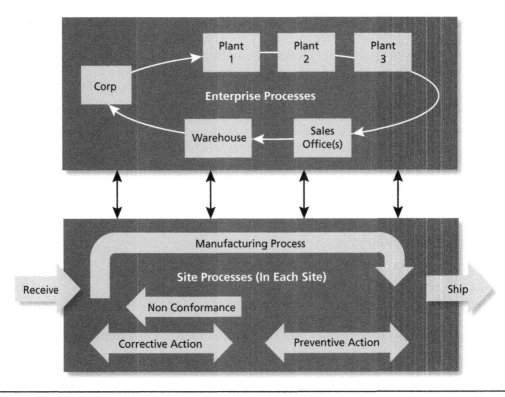

Figure 6.1 Enterprise process and site process interaction.

ENTERPRISE PROCESSES

Enterprise processes are the global processes linking corporate, design centers, sales, and manufacturing plants. They essentially provide linkages within the enterprise and they extend beyond the four walls of a site. Global process owners and enterprise process measurables typically measure important metrics such as on-time delivery, design lead time, and ppm rejects. They reflect the customer experience, especially if the process is classified as a customer oriented process (COP).

Note: Customer oriented processes are defined as processes that get an input from the customer with an output going back to the customer from the COP.

SITE PROCESSES

Site processes are confined to within the four walls of the organization. They are standardized globally, but their management and effect is primarily within the four walls of the site. These processes are important in their own right. They provide customers with the product (as well as all the supporting processes). Site processes include inspection/testing, warehousing, and other site-specific functions.

Implementing an integrated management system requires the organization to carefully design processes for maximum effectiveness. Enterprise and site processes are important design elements for an effective integrated management system. The process map and processes help the organization meet 4.1 General Requirements and 4.2 Documentation Requirements in the QMS, 4.4.4 Documentation in EMS and OHSMS, and 4.2 in Food Safety Management Systems (FSSC 22000).

In other words, the process map and the processes represent an integrated management system that fulfills the requirements and expectations of QMS, EMS, OHSMS, and FSMS in an organization.

The next building block is the performance management system of the organization.

DEVELOPING THE PERFORMANCE MANAGEMENT SYSTEM—OPERATING SYSTEM

The performance management system identifies the key performance indicators (KPIs) and the top process measurables.

The KPIs or key measurables are reviewed by top management in periodic (typically monthly) business reviews. The key measurables highlight the pulse of the organization and, if properly implemented, will reflect the organization's goals and objectives. The goals and objectives should be aligned with the organization's customer needs and expectations. See Figure 6.2.

Figure 6.2 Aligning interested parties/customer expectations, goals and objectives, and metrics.

Key processes are those that are correlated with the organization's key measurables. The key processes are measured using process measurables. Improved process measurables will help the organization improve the key measurable (the proper nomenclature in a BOS is a result measurable). This will help the organization meet its goals and objectives, which will in turn help to meet customer needs and expectations. An alignment chart helps link customer expectations with the goals and objectives of the organization and their performance system.

Figure 6.3 shows that if set up vacancies, unplanned schedule changes, machine downtime, and stockouts decrease, then percent on-time delivery will improve. This improvement will allow the organization to meets its strategic goals and objectives and also help meet customer delivery performance expectations.

In this manner, using alignment charts, the organization's result and process measurables are determined sequentially, one customer expectation category at a time. The measurables are documented using a business control plan as shown in Figure 6.4.

The performance management system is an important building block of the integrated management system, consisting not only of measurables or metrics, but also of regular monthly meetings, meeting agendas, and a continual improvement plan. Properly designed, the performance management system consists of a leadership team and improvement teams (ITs), as shown in Figure 6.5.

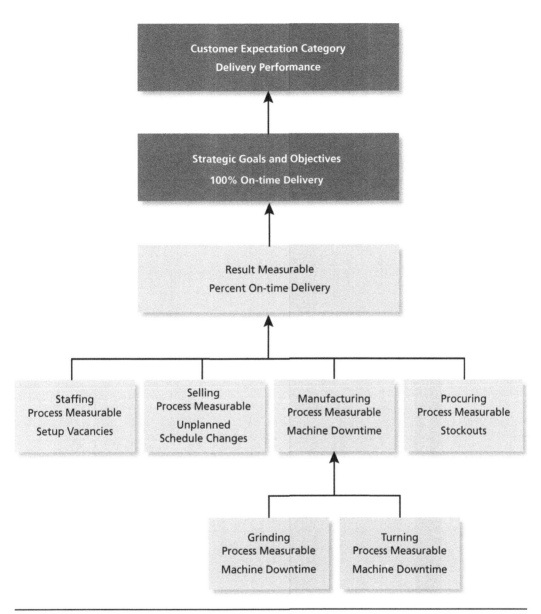

Figure 6.3 Goals and objectives alignment chart.

Process Activity	Customer Req/ Expectation	Key Process/ COP	Measurement	Responsibility	Acceptance Criteria 2002 Q1, Q2, Q3, Q4	Review Frequency	Control Methods	Comments/ Reaction
				EXAMPLES				
Business Fulfillment	On-time delivery	K	% On-time in operations	Logistics	94, 95, 96, 96%	4/yr	Monthly management meeting	Corrective action after 3 consecutive
			% on-time to customer	Production control	100%	4/yr	Trend chart	C/A is more than 15% off target
Customer Complaint	Provide timely response	C	Complaint response	Quality	10 days	4/Yr	Production control dept	Continue to monitor
Design & Development	Meet timing requirement		Time to market	Design/dev	52 weeks	Weekly	Quality department	R, Y, G reaction
Business Creation	Innovation		Patents filed	Design	20 per year	Monthly	Design meeting	Continue to monitor

Business Management System Control Plan

Organization: _____

General Manager: _____

Product Description: _____

Issue/Rev Date: _____

Figure 6.4 Business management system control plan.

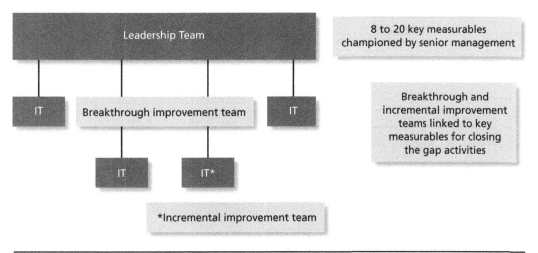

Figure 6.5 A performance management system.

Data management standards using disciplined presentation methods such as a four panel chart or a business balanced score card can be used, as shown in Figures 6.6 and 6.7.

Figure 6.6, a four-panel chart, shows the relationship between the trend chart, the Pareto showing the vital few improvements that need to be worked on, and the action plans of the improvement team. The Paynter chart is a technique used in the automotive industry to ensure the actions are resulting in improvements.

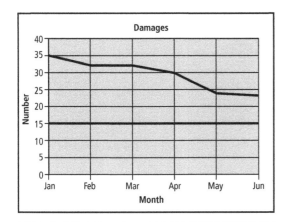

Figure 6.6 Four panel chart.

The performance management system is a building block in the integrated management system. The goal is not just to measure performance but to rapidly improve the organization to meet and exceed customer expectations. The model of the performance management system is shown in Figure 6.7.

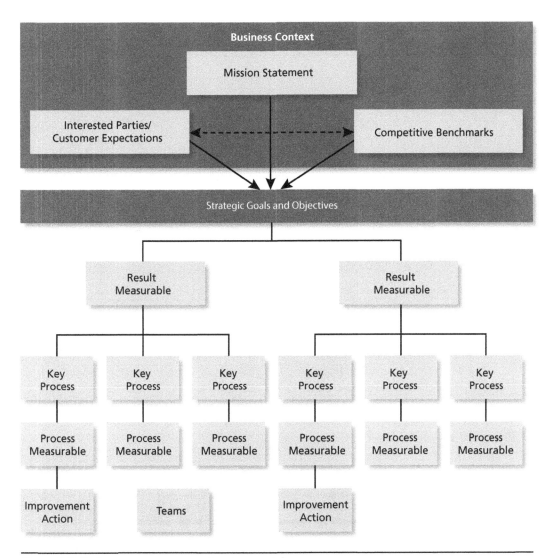

Figure 6.7 Performance management system model.

The integration of Lean and Six Sigma with a performance management system is shown in Figure 6.8.

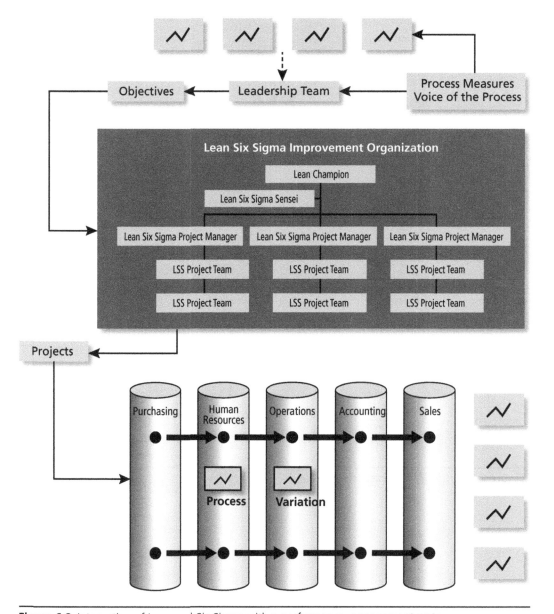

Figure 6.8 Integration of Lean and Six Sigma with a performance management system.

The performance management system satisfies the requirements of 5.2 Customer Focus, 5.4 Planning, 5.6 Management Review, and 8.5.1 Continual Improvement Plan in ISO 9001. It also satisfies the requirements of 4.3.3 Objectives, Targets and Program, 4.5.1 Monitoring and Measurement (partial), and Management Review (4.6) in ISO 14001 and ISO 45001. It also satisfies objectives in 5.1 Management Commitment, 5.3 Food Safety Management System Planning, 5.8 Management Review, and 8.5.1 Continual Improvement in FSSC 22000.

New Product Development (NPD)

Another important building block in an integrated management system is the new product development process. Keep in mind that the product could be hardware, software, processed material, or a service. Some important linked processes include sales and the contract review, during which customer requirements are first understood directly from the customer. The NPD process includes project management and planning, product and process design, a first article inspection (FAI), and a production part approval process (PPAP). The FAI and PPAP help ensure that all requirements are being met. Furthermore, the process design includes gates and gate reviews in addition to project reviews. Gate reviews are attended by top management who are coached to conduct reviews and determine whether the product can move forward to the next phase in the process.

Preventive and risk management techniques are built into both product and process design using FMEAs to determine Q, E, HS, and FS risks, as discussed in Chapter 3. See Figure 6.9.

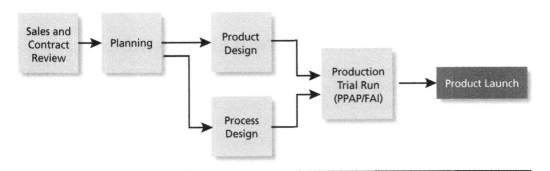

Figure 6.9 Preventive and risk management techniques.

The sales and contract review process is detailed below. The planning process is led by a program or project manager with a planning checklist that goes from the project proposal to PPAP or FAI and post launch review. Keep in mind that best in class requires a cross-functional team as core members of the project team. The product design process involves Design FMEA including quality, environmental, and health and safety risk assessments (Q, E, HS) and/or HACCP (food safety) risk assessments in the product design phase. The process design phase includes conducting process FMEA and EHS aspects/impact/hazard analysis during manufacturing design. The production trial run includes operator training, conducting measurement systems analysis and process capability. The final gate is the FAI or PPAP, where a dimensional report of all characteristics and final validation is performed, ensuring customer requirements can be met by the actual production process.

Sales and Contract Review

This process takes place when the request for quote process is received and the quote is processed. The review ensures that the organization can meet all customer requirements including quality and delivery. In best in class processes, the organization works with the customer to define the critical product characteristics or product elements. The contract review stage sets the stage for the NPD process since the initial assumptions and costing casts a heavy shadow on product development. How much planning and risk prevention/analysis needs to take place at this stage is a decision made based on the uniqueness of the product and the potential opportunity (that is, revenue and risk). Many organizations will perform a manufacturing feasibility study at the contract stage to ensure manufacturing provides its input in terms of the manufacturability of the customer proposal.

MANUFACTURING PROCESS CONTROL

Manufacturing processes should be designed using process flow, PFMEAs, control plans, and linked work instructions as shown in Figure 6.10. The manufacturing line needs a lean flow meeting the customer demand (or Takt time). The manufacturing process was designed and the production trail run was completed in the new product development process during the process design phase. Another element of the process design is the methodology for design for manufacturing and design for assembly (DFM/DFA).

Factories designed with risk prevention tools following risk based control plans and inspection sheets with error/mistake proofing are able to have 60 PPM or less of external/customer errors.

The three processes of the performance based system, new product development, and manufacturing process control are the key processes to the overall success of an organization. Design and implementation to a best in class level takes time and effort.

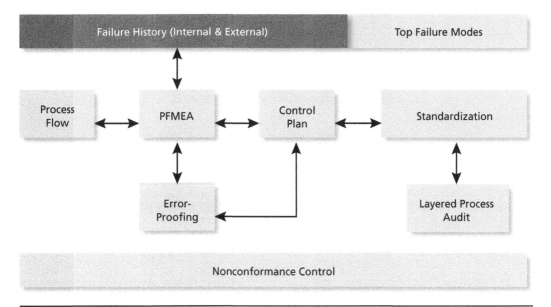

Figure 6.10 Manufacturing process control design.

RISK AND CHANGE MANAGEMENT

This is a product and process change process (including engineering change) that differentiates between major and minor change. Major change needs to go through a cross-functional review and a manage-the-change checklist. The change checklist lists all the documents, gages, tooling, FMEAs, control plans, and work instructions that could be changed. It also asks whether a PPAP or FAI should be conducted. In many industries this process also triggers a customer communication of the change.

Problem Solving

This is the company's corrective action process and includes customer, supplier, and internal problems as inputs. This is a very important process for the overall success of the organization. Best in class methods call for a disciplined methodology using cross-functional teams for major/critical company issues. See the flow chart illustrated in Figure 6.11. Best in class methods call for a review of FMEAs to help identify the cause and also to update the FMEAs as one of the last steps of the problem solving process.

Internal Auditing

The internal auditing process should be an enterprise process as detailed in Chapter 5. The company can perform several types of processes including system, product, manufacturing, and layered process audits. This is the subject of book two in the series on integrated management systems.

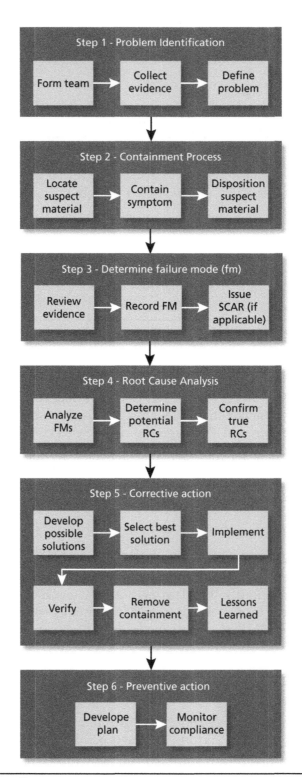

Figure 6.11 Steps for effective problem solving.

Enterprise Document Management and Records Management

This should be conducted via an enterprise software that is able to manage all the documents in an enterprise. The organization should be able to view the documents as integrated, quality, environmental, and health/safety or food safety, or by each function. The management system documentation should be available as needed by the organization. Further, the level IV forms should be available for the organization to complete, route for approval, and review. After approval they should become records in the same system.

SUMMARY

Integrated management systems implemented as a concept or a mantra may not be enough. There is much latitude in how a process is designed and implemented. While there is much gained by implementing an enterprise-wide integrated management system, this chapter explains that the design of processes is key to overall success. This chapter will be the basis of the third book in the series about designing and implementing best in class processes in an integrated management system.

7

Integration with GFSI Standards in the Food Industry

A few years ago, a 150-year-old bakery that sold goods primarily via mail order contacted us to help them implement GFSI standards. After much discussion of the different GFSI standards, they settled on FSSC 22000. This was in the beginning stages of FSSC, even before the market knew that most major food organizations would finally adopt this standard. We will call this company Old Bakery. Old Bakery had three facilities, two that did the baking and another that assembled the goods into a customer offering. Their focus was the oldest bakery and they wanted to exclude the assembly plant that was under the supervision and control of the bakery management. Also, they wanted to scope out the mail order business that supported sales.

Note

FSSC 22000 includes the following standards or methodologies: ISO22000, ISO 20002-1, and HACCP. ISO 22000 is a food safety management system that has been accepted by the International Organization of Standardization. Associated with ISO 220000 is a prerequisite program, ISO 20002-1, which was previously a British Standards Institute PAS 220 standard. Prerequisites in the food industry refer to Good Manufacturing practices (GMPs) that food manufacturers should implement. Additionally, FSSC 220000 addresses food safety risks via a methodology called Hazard Analysis and Critical Control Points (HACCP). More on HACCP is provided in Chapter 4.

Since the bakery and the mail order business were the oldest businesses, there was a lot of interest from top management in this implementation. The organization had a quality and food safety system, but they were aware that it did not comply with ISO 9001 or GFSI standards. They had many different assessments from multiple customers during a year including an AIB (American Institute of Baking) audit for bakeries. The authors conducted an initial assessment of the factory and advised them to go for FSSC 22000 and ISO 9001 in the same implementation.

In our opinion, when implementing a GFSI system for food safety, quality systems come for free (based on similarity of requirements). Some of the major findings in our initial assessment were as follows:

- The performance management system had major issues:
  - Business objectives covering the quality, delivery, efficiency, and food safety requirements were not available.
  - Business reviews covering the topics required by FSSC 22000 and ISO 9001:2008 were not evident.
  - Quality and food safety policy statements covering the requirements of 5.3 (ISO 9001) and 5.2 (ISO 22000) were not available.
- Customer feedback in various forms was available but not used:
  - Focus groups
  - Online surveys
  - Customer comments
  - Market research and
  - Statistical comments
  - There was no formal process for how this information is used for strategic planning and / or product innovations (that is, there was need for more analysis and use of the data gathered).
  - Customer satisfaction / customer input data were not available to the organization and management from the new direct sales (supermarket) segment.
  - Information from trade shows, sales calls, call logs, surveys, and customer comments was not shared with management.
- There was no documented procedure for document and records control.
- Many documents were not in the document control system.
- Some departments (such as HR) developed their own intranet to manage documents, resulting in an overall loss of documentation control).
- A comprehensive record retention matrix was not available.
- The recall process, SOP 14, was inadequate.
  - The documented process did not show authority for persons executing the withdrawal.
  - Furthermore, the procedure did not specify "who" or "what" provides "notification to relevant authorities" or handles product withdrawals or the sequence of actions taken.

- The HACCP program had some major deficiencies, including:
  - No standing food safety (HACCP) team
  - Not all required information available
  - Available required information scattered over multiple documents
  - Information not tied together
  - Complexity introduced by inefficiencies
  - Multiple uses of terms; lack of consistency
- Documentation of prerequisite programs (PRP) was incomplete as compared to ISO/TS 22002-1. Some issues noted:
  - Discussion of cracks in joints where food can get trapped
  - Overhead utility as a source of contamination (need verification of PRP controls)
  - Wash areas that do not have signage of hand wash requirements
  - Food Code requirements for illness and sickness of visitors and employees not implemented (FDA Model Forms Annex 7)
- The new product development planning process showed that project managers were assigned; however, they had not formally documented a timing chart of activities and overall program goals.
- No consistent product development process was followed, as evidenced by the sampling of three products that were recently introduced.
- Products sampled showed a lack of detailed design input for requirements such as moisture level, final packaging, dimension taste, and others.
- There was no formal design review documentation/record.
- There was no formal documentation of the pilot runs and no conclusion that design input meets design output.
- There was no feedback and corrective action loop to improve processes.
- Manufacturing processes (shop paper, recipe cards, and inspection sheets) were the documentation used to determine process controls on the baking line. There were several problems:
  - The readings made by the operator to set up the line were not recorded.
  - Supervisors were not aware of the critical control points (CCP) on the baking line.
  - For one product number, the weight control reports showed limits of 1.08 to 1.18; however, the product was running between 1.18 and 1.23.
  - The Upfront and Main Bakeries did not have formal final inspection requirements (before pack).

- – Production floor had wood splinters from the wooden pallets strewn in many areas.
  - – There was no metal detector in the final packaging line, although there was such at the end of the bake line.
- In addition there were problems with training/competency and much more...

The implementation plan recommended by the authors and agreed to is illustrated in Figure 7.1. It shows the development of level I and then level II documents. The level I documents are typically developed by the authors working with the implementation leader. Level II is developed with process owners and cross functional process teams. The authors conducted two-day facilitations for teams to create rough drafts of the procedures and helped Old Bakery develop their process documentation in these two-day events. In addition to the process documentation, several initiatives to improve the organization were undertaken.

a. Improve performance management system using Omnex BOS process.

b. Develop HACCP using a food safety team in what the authors call a process review by product families. Integrate risk analysis for food and quality in the HACCP analysis (see also Chapter 4).

c. Introduce a change management process for product and process change.

d. Develop a new product development phase gate process that includes top management reviews to assure development activities (including preventive activities) are completed successfully and on time. (The Omnex new product development process with HACCP analysis was introduced in Old Bakery.)

e. Implement disciplined problem solving to improve quality; introduce escape, occur, and system root causes and 5 Why analysis.

f. Recommend 5S and assist Old Bakery to do this with a grant from a local community college with another organization.

The goal of the implementation was not only to achieve FSSC 22000 certification but also to achieve overall improvement. One of the improvement goals was to reduce overall defectives from approximately 2% to 1.5%. This number included complaints and returned product. Old Bakery suffered from a problem that the author has viewed in multiple organizations (that is, accepting the present level of defectives as the best that they could achieve). When presented with the data, several persons in the quality and food safety organization mentioned that people only complained to get free product. Acceptance of the status quo was the biggest deterrent to improvement.

Many companies make certification the goal, rather than making improvement the goal and achieving certification as the byproduct. In fact, the authors' message to senior management in the executive overview was to make the effort improvement oriented versus just certification.

FSSC 22000 and ISO 9001:2008 Implementation Plan

Who		Feb	Mar	Apr	May	Jun	Jul	Aug	Sep	Oct	Nov	Dec
Implementation Leader	Conduct Assessment	X										
Implementation Leader	Form Implementation Team		X									
	Level I Policy Manual		Draft	Final								
Process Owners	Develop Process Documentation		X (Two 2-day events)	X								
HACCP Team	HACCP Development		X	X	X							
HACCP Team	Develop Pre Requisite Program		X	X	X							
HACCP Team	Update Employee Manual		X	X	X							
Implementation Leader	Choose Registrar			X								
Top Management Team	BOS			X	X							
Process Owner	Change Management			X	X							
Process Owner/CFT	NPD - Phased Launch Process			X	X							
Problem Solving Owner and Problem Solving Teams	Disciplined Problem Solving			X	X							
Outside Omnex Scope	5 S											
Omnex	Documentation Review					X						
Process Owners	Roll Out of Documentation					X						
Internal Auditors	Internal Auditor Training					X						
Internal Auditors	Internal Audit/Corrective Action					X		X				
Registrar	3rd Party Audit								X			

Figure 7.1 Integrated implementation plan for quality and food safety.

All IMS implementations are large changes within an organization. It is sometimes difficult enough to just get well integrated documentation and have it implemented and audited that the improvement focus could become waylaid.

DOCUMENTATION DEVELOPMENT

Level I Quality Manual and the Process Approach

The table of contents for the level I manual is shown in Figure 7.2. The authors often refer to the level I manual as a BMS manual or a policy manual, so as not to identify it as a functional manual belonging to either the quality or food safety functions. In 4.2.2 of ISO 9001, the quality manual requirements are evident as the "interaction of the processes," scope statement, and either the processes or the reference to the processes. These three requirements can easily be fulfilled in two pages. The manual shown below goes beyond the requirements of ISO 9001. The goal of this manual is to do much more; in fact, this manual is meant to be updated and circulated yearly. It is meant to be a marketing document for the organization.

Readers should be interested in the process map illustrated in Figure 7.3. Each process map shown for the six companies in this manual is unique since each company is different. The key point to be made is that there are three key process groups that make an organization what it is: performance management (as an audit trail for auditing we often refer to this as business planning and management review), new product development with its phase gate reviews, and the bakery process (including the process control for quality and food safety).

Contents

I. Introduction to Old Bakery

II. Vision and Mission Statement

III. Quality Policy

IV. Food Safety Policy

V. Scope of the ISO 9001:2008 and FSSC 22000 Implementation

VI. Products – Old Bakery

VII. Process Map – Old Bakery

VIII. Process List

IX. BMS Control Plan

X. Corporate and Plant Management Meetings

XI. Description of the Food Safety and Management Systems

XII. Pre-requisite Program and ISO/TS 22002 Checklist

Figure 7.2 Level I manual table of contents.

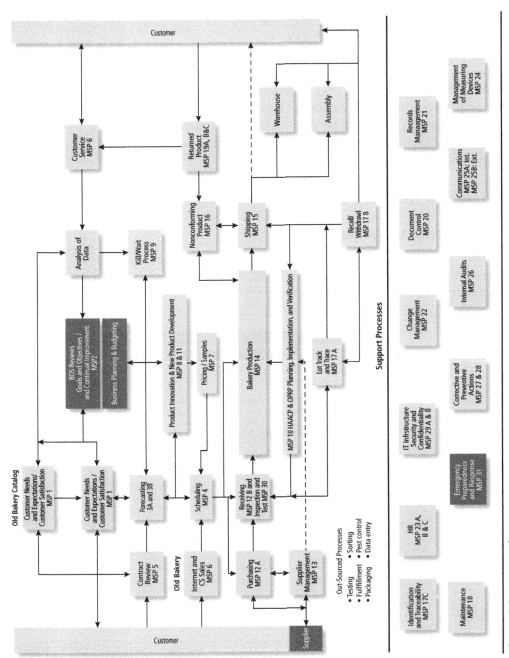

Figure 7.3 Integrated process map.

The color brown is used to show processes that are outside the scope and red for processes that are food safety alone. All other processes are integrated and satisfy both ISO 9001 and FSSC 22000.

The processes were developed by process owners who were responsible for process measurables and the development and implementation of their processes. This is an important step for both food safety and quality (that is, ensuring that the ownership of quality and food safety is companywide). It is worth remarking that environmental and health and safety are sometimes narrowly and functionally managed; EHS will benefit from the creation of process owners and the enterprise wide roll out.

PROCESS IMPROVEMENTS FROM THE IMPLEMENTATION

Performance Management

Old Bakery profited greatly with the addition of the business operating system (BOS). Old Bakery adopted the following key measurables based on customer expectations.

Measurable (Performance Characteristic)
Innovation
Profitability
Efficiencies
Delivery (fulfillment)
Product / Service Quality
Food Quality
Product Cost
Value of Stockholders
Customer Satisfaction
Productivity
Food Safety
Employee Satisfaction

The new paradigm made champions responsible for a score card with performance expectations. The old style was to review financial indicators at the end of each month. Old Bakery adopted the BOS methodology wholeheartedly including trend charts with goal lines, Pareto analysis, improvement plans, and a Paynter chart. By the time the authors disengaged, the company had started making improvements in key measurables.

Management Review

As per the requirements of QMS and FSMS, management review requires more than just a review of the business key measurables. Even though the key measurable includes the key food and quality objectives, the standards require more. Management review can cover all the requirements monthly or look at the less important ideas quarterly or every six months. The management review agenda conducted monthly included the following agenda items:

Inputs (agenda items) for Food Safety & Quality Management Systems Management Review

1. Follow up actions from previous management review
2. BOS measures of food safety and quality
   a. Number of customer complaints
   b. Supplier rejects
   c. Injury/illness incidents
   d. Delivery % on-time
   e. Premium freight – rush shipments
3. Results of audits
   a. Internal
   b. External
   c. Planned verification activities
   d. Inspections
4. Customer feedback
   a. Returns
   b. Customer satisfaction surveys
   c. External communication activities
5. Status of preventive and corrective actions
6. Changes that could affect the food safety and quality management system
   a. Changed circumstances
   b. System changes
7. Recommended improvement projects/actions and resource requirements
   a. Product quality
   b. Product safety

PROCESS IMPROVEMENTS

Integrating Quality and Food Safety

As noted in Chapter 4, HACCP and the FMEA process originated during the same time for the same reason (that is, NASA launch of the first space vehicle). Both enjoy the same thought processes. The authors integrate both quality and food safety around the HACCP process. There are some differences between the two methodologies: FMEAs are used to identify and control all characteristics (automotive industry implementation) while HACCP only controls the critical control points (CCPs). Typically, industries new to using FMEA (for example, aerospace) also start initially controlling only critical characteristics. (See Table 7.1 for an example of HACCP used to control quality and food safety at Old Bakery.) This HACCP was developed using a cross functional food safety team using the Omnex process review methodology that analyzes risk by product families.

Table 7.1 shows that the CCP can be figured out based on the HACCP flow chart; other significant characteristics can be based on the severity and overall residual risk number calculated based on the RPN or risk priority number (Sev x Occ x Det).

In food safety it is important to distinguish between CCPs and significant characteristics since the CCPs violations or shipments have to be reported to the FDA.

The HACCP leads to linked documents that detail the controls needed within the organization. In most industries only the CCPs are controlled. In other industries all characteristics are controlled, not just CCPs or the characteristics we identified in the HACCP as significant. In Table 7.2 we show an inspection plan that identifies all characteristics for the operator on the Old Bakery. From the HACCP plan an inspection sheet can be used for the operator, a PRP sheet for a PRP audit, and/or preventive maintenance plan for maintenance.

Table 7.1 HACCP food safety and quality for Old Bakery.

Process Step	Food Safety and Quality Requirements	Failure Modes or Malfunction	Food Safety Hazards or Quality Effect	Sev	Cause	Preventive Controls	Occ	Detective Controls:	Det	RPN
Old Bakery (Cheesecake Filling)	No biological hazards	Pathogen in raw or excess material	Fever, diarrhea	8	From supplier	PRP: Supplier Management	2	PRP: Receiving Inspection	7	112
					Improper storage and handling of excess material	Temp controlled storage	2	PRP: Inbound Inspection	7	112
					Build up in machine crevices due to improper cleaning	PRP: Sanitation; testing via environmental audits	2	Visual inspection	8	128
	No chemical hazards	Contamination from cleaning agents	No discernable effect	1	Improper cleaning	PRP: Sanitation	3	None	10	30
		Contamination from machine oil	No discernable effect; use of food grade oil	1	Seal failure	use of food grade oil; PRP: PM	1	Visual observation	8	8
	No Physical Hazards	Plastic	Choking hazard	10	Broken plastic guard	PRP: PM program	5	Visual observation	8	400
		Metal	Broken tooth, choking hazard	10	Paddle to bowl contact; misc machine hardware above bowl		2	Visual observation during processing; EOL: metal detector (CCP)	8	160
	Smooth consistency	Lumpy	Scrap, process interruption	8	Inconsistent tempering of cream cheese		2	Visual observation	8	128
					Adding multiple ingredients at same time	Work aid	3	Visual observation	8	192
	Proper cupweight	Too heavy	Excessive cost per product	5	Failure to follow recipe/ work instructions		5	Weight measurements at setup	5	125
		Too light	Under weight – label violation	8	Failure to follow recipe/ work instructions		5	Weight measurements at setup	5	200
	Uniform distribution of chocolate liquor	Chips of chocolate	Scrap	8	Failure to follow recipe/ work instructions		3	Visual observation	8	192

Table 7.2 Operator inspection plan.

Description	Requirement	Control Method	Gage	1	2	3	Other...
OP #30 Cheese Cake Filling	No Plastic/ look for broken plastic guard	Visual inspection	None				
	Paddle to bowl contact	Visual inspection	None				
	Lumpy/temperature 75°	Checksheet	Temperature gage				
	Cup weight .3 grams	Checksheet	Scale				
	Uniform distribution of chips	Visual inspection	None				

DEVELOPING A NEW PRODUCT DEVELOPMENT PHASE GATE PROCESS

Omnex introduced its new product development process without DFMEAs in Old Bakery. The initial audit had showed no defined process for developing new products. Defining the process with quality and food safety helped this process immensely. Suddenly, products started moving much faster from R&D and the lab to the bakery. Most importantly, due to a well-defined validation process for the design or recipe, products successfully moved from design to production.

Disciplined Problem Solving

The authors conducted training for disciplined problem solving and helped Old Bakery understand problems, root causes, and corrective and preventive actions. They had started implementing this methodology, but this process had not become institutionalized in the organization. One of their success stories was solving a listeria problem that had plagued the organization. The problem solving team traced the problem to a machine design issue and they redesigned the process.

However, without customer requirements for the rigor required and because the organization lacked trained facilitators, this process is probably not something that took root.

AUDITS

Two internal audits were conducted. The first one was led by the authors and the results were typical of most of the internal audits conducted in an implementation, the discovery that there was still much to do in the system. The first internal audit is typically a "wake up call" for the process owners and the management that there is "much to do and that they need to focus" and spend dedicated time to implement the system.

When process owners are assigned processes that are aligned to their daily work, then there is self-interest to ensure those processes are understood and effectively implemented. Also, with integration, there is no special process for Quality, Environmental or Health and Safety; there is only one management system and it is focused on business processes of the organization.

The key lesson learned by process owners in an audit, especially if they have never been taken through an ISO style audit, is the need to keep records and to monitor and improve their processes. This was certainly the lesson learned by Old Bakery.

THIRD-PARTY AUDIT

Old Bakery was finally ready for the assessment after the second audit. The idea of having records and objective evidence for each of the processes had been driven home. Many of the processes, including the performance management, problem solving, and new product development, were new and immature. There was definitely risk remaining in the management system.

Old Bakery conducted a second internal audit. The two audits and corrective action cycles had made their impact. The system was now ready for the third-party audit, which was a big success. The auditor was laudatory of the system that had been designed. Old Bakery was certified on the first try with a few minor nonconformances.

8

Integration in an Automotive Organization

The company chosen in this case study is an Asia-based automotive tier-one supplier with a corporate facility and five plants spread out throughout this large country (see Figure 8.1). One has to fly between the plants because none of the factories are within driving distance of the others.

The corporate location housed central planning, purchasing, supply development, corporate HR, and top management. Each plant included the following functions: plant management, HR, indirect purchasing, and manufacturing.

The authors planned the implementation with corporate. Before starting the IMS implementation, the organization was introduced to Omnex through the training courses we had conducted for them. During the training sessions they quickly realized that their APQP, core tools methodology, and knowledge needed strengthening, even though they were already ISO/TS 16949 certified.

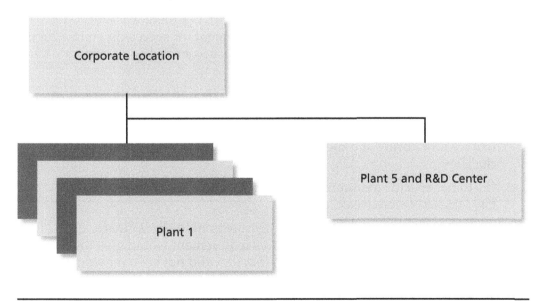

Figure 8.1 Automotive tier-one supplier case study.

During the same time we were working with them on the core tools under-standing, corporate wanted to implement both ISO 14001 and OHSAS 18001. We worked with them to understand the benefits of integrating quality, environmental, and health and safety management systems. Corporate quickly grasped the benefits of integration and had us train top management and present the overall strategy to their executive management for their concurrence. After the presentation, the president of the organization decided to work with Omnex to integrate ISO/TS 16949, ISO 14001, and OHSAS 18001 and including SA 8000 (a widely used social responsibility standard that originated in the textile industries in 1997).

Status of the Management System

Each of the plants and corporate were ISO/TS 16949 certified, but each site had separate quality manuals, procedures, and work instructions including forms and checklists. The implemented ISO/TS 16949 management system was weak, especially in the application of the core tools—APQP, FMEA, SPC, MSA, and PPAP standards.

EMS, OHSAS, and SA 8000 had no management systems and had to be implemented from scratch. We agreed to conduct an initial assessment to ISO 14001, OHSAS 18001, and SA 8000.

Here were the challenges in this implementation:

1. There was a lack of strong leadership in the corporate function driving the integration. We had top management support, but there was a need for continual push from executive top management for success in an integrated management system. More could have been accomplished if corporate had taken a stronger role in implementation.

2. Deploying objectives within a site had its challenges since the organization was very functionally oriented. Identifying the top level objectives and then working with functional managers and having them understand their role for monitoring and measuring for Q, E, and HS consistently was a challenge.

3. Customer specific requirements and core tools implementation for ISO/TS 16949 were weak.

4. SA 8000 had a collective bargaining requirement in the standard. Management in the plants felt that this requirement would give the union extra ammunition and involvement that they did not have previously and the decision was made not to go for SA 8000.

5. Some of the unionized plants were lax in the implementation of personal protective equipment (PPE) because the union viewed PPE as a hindrance rather than a help for their membership. The Union was not willing to make changes. In fact, in the middle of the implementation there was a strike in two of the plants unrelated to the IMS implementation.

6. Compliance to legal requirements was very poor due to poor enforcement from the local government.

Positives

Top management was very cooperative in each of the sites. This support came from a half-day training session for each of the general managers and their direct reports. They stayed a strong advocate for the integration of the management systems. The next tier of management, including process owners, senior managers, and managers, were trained in a four-day class focused on each of the standards and on the integration methodology. The management team, which was fairly young, embraced this approach.

Initial Assessment

An initial assessment was performed in each of the factories. Typical results are shown in Figure 8.2. The initial assessment of SA 8000 showed that there were no policies or procedures or awareness of social accountability in this large and sophisticated automotive organization. In fact, a spider web would place many requirements close to a zero.

Based on the initial assessment, an implementation plan was formed as shown in Table 8.1.

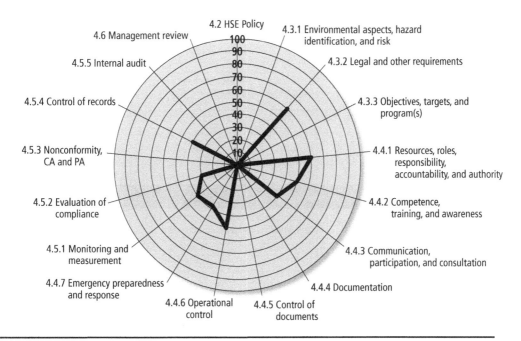

Figure 8.2 Degree of conformance to integrated management system.

Table 8.1 Implementation plan.

Updated on:	November 10, 2014
Revision number:	0
Type T refers to	TRAINING
Type C refers to	CONSULTING
Total Mandays required	132

No.	Activity	Deliverables	Location	Type	Duration
1	Initial assessment of documentation and systems to obtain a clear understanding of existing management system (TS 16949) and identify specific gaps w.r.t. ISO 14001, OHSAS 18001, and SA 8000.	GAP analysis report consisting of requirement vs availability – Recommendations with implementation plan – Assess requirements for integrating it with existing TS 16949 documents/ systems	1	C	1
			2	C	2
			3	C	1
			4	C	1
			5	C	1
2	Top management orientation, to explain the scope of integrated management system, the relation between business and IMS implementation and to explain the concept of IMS.	Top management support – Foundation for IMS implementation – Agreement on road map and resource requirement – Policy guidelines to top management	1	C	2
			2		
			3		
			4		
			5		
3	Establishing policies. Develop an integrated policy based on initial review, organizational needs, existing policies, and requirements of standards.	Policy drafting and approval from management and release.	1	C	2
			2		
			3		
			4		
			5		
A	PILLAR – 1, Policy Development and Deployment		TOLL GATE REVIEW		
4	Awareness program	Requirements of ISO 14001, OHSAS 18001, and SA 8000 standards are explained	1		
			2	T	4
			3	T	4
			4		
			5		
5	Training on identification of aspect and impacts and hazard and risk	Team trained on the process analysis to – Conduct aspect/impact study using E-FMEA – Conduct hazard identification and risk assessment using S-FMEA – Other requirements specific to ISO 14001, OHSAS 18001, and SA 8000 at each location – Guidance for document review	1	T	1
			2	T	2
			3	T	2
			4	T	2
			5	T	2

(Continued)

Table 8.1 Implementation plan. *(Continued)*

No.	Activity	Deliverables	Location	Type	Duration
6	Review of documentation on aspect/impact study and risk/ hazard identification	All plants have identified – Aspects and impacts – Verification of aspect impact for their adequacy – Guidance for identifying the significant aspects/ hazards – Guidance is identifying and drafting the action – Review of documents for adequacy	1	C	2
			2	C	3
			3	C	3
			4	C	2
			5	C	2
B	**PILLAR – 2, Finalize Documentation for Aspects and Impacts**		**TOLL GATE REVIEW**		
7	Training on legal requirements and emergency preparedness plan	Team trained on legal requirements pertaining to – ISO 14001, OHSAS 18001, and SA 8000 – Other requirements specific to ISO 14001, OHSAS 18001, and SA 8000 at each location – Training on emergence preparedness plan – Guidance for document review	1		
			2	T	2
			3	T	2
			4		
			5	T	2
8	Review of legal compliance and emergency preparedness plan	Legal requirements are reviewed and verified – Legal register released – Legal requirements compliance calendar released across the organization – All onsite emergency plans reviewed for adequacy and suitability. – Emergency preparedness plan has been released for implementation	1		
			2	C	3
			3	C	3
			4	C	2
			5	C	2
C	**PILLAR – 3, Finalize documentation for Risk/Hazard Analysis**		**TOLL GATE REVIEW**		
9	Assist in development of IMS manual as per Standards requirements and integrating to the existing TS documents	Review of existing documentation – Categorization by process for inclusion whenever possible – Document and data control – Categorize documentation as Level 1, 2, or 3 – Distribution of documentation to implementation teams	1	C	3
			2	C	6
			3	C	6
			4	C	4
			5	C	5
D	**PILLAR – 4, Finalize IMS Manual**		**TOLL GATE REVIEW**		
10	Review of all documents and control plans	Review and release of – Corporate and unit level IMS manual – Process level IMS manual – Process documents – Control plans – Well-defined process objectives and measures, targets – Review programs and operational control procedures	1	C	2
			2	C	4
			3	C	4
			4	C	3
			5	C	3

(Continued)

Table 8.1 Implementation plan. *(Continued)*

No.	Activity	Deliverables	Location	Type	Duration
11	Internal auditors training	Selected members trained and qualified for auditing the organization's EMS, OHSAS, and SA 8000 – Development of internal audit questions for all procedures – Development of audit check sheets	1		
			2	T	5
			3	T	5
			4		
			5		
E	PILLAR – 5, Release of All Documentation		TOLL GATE REVIEW		
12	Conduct internal audits with internal auditors	Sample internal audits performed before the pre-assessment and after the pre-assessment with the internal auditors – Sample audits conducted with the internal auditors – Understanding the internal auditing process – Guidelines for writing the scope and purpose, obtaining audit evidence – Guidelines for writing non-conformity report, reporting audit results, and follow-up	1	C	1
			2	C	4
			3	C	3
			4	C	2
			5	C	2
13	Management review support	Support provided to conduct one management review for EMS and OHSAS satisfying the standard requirements	1	C	1
			2	C	1
			3	C	1
			4	C	1
			5	C	1
F	PILLAR – 6, Conducting Internal Audit		TOLL GATE REVIEW		
14	Support to close any gaps identified during audit	Support provided to close all gaps identified in the pre-assessment audits	1	C	2
			2	C	2
			3	C	2
			4	C	2
			5	C	2
G	PILLAR – 7, Gap Closing		TOLL GATE REVIEW		

The quality manual designed for this organization was clause oriented. In other words, organized around the clauses of ISO/TS 16949 (QMS). Especially when integrating all three standards, it is best to abandon a clause orientation. In many ways the level I manual reads like a QMS manual that is based on the old ISO 9001 standard based on the 1994 revision which was not process based. This indeed was found to be the origin of this document. As shown in the table of contents (Figure 8.3), the quality manual includes an integrated process map, lists all of the procedures, and includes work instructions and forms/checklists. Again, this level of detail is not best for the level I manual.

Level I Manual

TABLE OF CONTENTS

Section **Contents** **Page No.**

Figure 8.3 Level 1 manual table of contents.

Enterprise Procedures

Consultants worked to standardize 41 procedures companywide (Table 8.2). These were deemed corporate procedures and all plants adopted them. Some of these processes did not have a one-to-one relationship with the process map of the organization. Note: This is a typical problem found in organizations where the linkage between the process map processes and the process documentation in level II do not fully match.

Table 8.2 Standardized enterprise procedures.

a. Corporate Processes		
SI No.	Document No.	Document Name
1	CORP\CT\Process\01	New Product development
2	CORP\CT\Process\02	Product Design Change
3	CORP\CT\Process\03	Analysis of customer complaint—OEM
4	CORP\CT\Process\04	Analysis of Field complaint—Replacement
5	CORP\CT\Process\05	Production part approval process
6	CORP\CT\Process\06	Manufacturing Process Design
7	CORP\CT\Process\07	Process Design Changes
8	CORP\D&D\Process\01	Selection and approval of Mould suppliers
9	CORP\D&D\Process\02	Inspection, Acceptance and Release of Final Products
10	CORP\D&D\Process\03	Re-qualification of Mold vendors and capability development
11	CORP\D&D\Process\04	Provision of Test center services
12	CORP\R&D\Process\01	Approval of raw materials from new sources
13	CORP\R&D\Process\02	New compound development
14	CORP\TS\Process\01	Customer complaint handling process—Replacements.
15	CORP\TS\Process\02	Customer complaint handling process—Institutional
16	CORP\TS\Process\03	Calibration of service equipments
17	CORP\TS\Process\04	Product evaluation
18	CORP\TS\Process\05	Claim Re-inspection process
19	CORP\PUR\Process\01	Purchasing of Raw Materials & bought out products
20	CORP\PUR\Process\02	New source approval & development
21	CORP\PUR\Process\03	Assessment & development of existing suppliers
22	CORP\PRO\Process\01	Procurement & commissioning of capital equipment
23	CORP\MKT\Process\01	Customer need identification
24	CORP\MKT\Process\02	Sales Process—Institutional
25	CORP\MKT\Process\03	Sales Process—Replacement
26	CORP\MKT\Process\04	Measurement & monitoring of customer satisfaction
27	CORP\MKT\Process\05	Receipt, Handling, Storage & Dispatch of products—Dos
28	CORP\HR\Process\01	Recruitment

(Continued)

Table 8.2 Standardized enterprise procedures. *(Continued)*

Sl No.	Document No.	Document Name
29	CORP\HR\Process\02	Training
30	CORP\HR\Process\03	Employee motivation & empowerment
31	CORP\HR\Process\04	Performance appraisal
32	CORP\SCM\Process\01	Production planning and control
33	CORP\SCM\Process\02	Delivery of products
34	CORP\SCM\Process\03	Receipt, Handling, Storage & Dispatch of products— RDC's & OE Godowns
b. General Procedures		
Sl No.	Document No.	Document Name
1	CORP / CMR / Procedure / 01	Document and Data Control
2	CORP / CMR / Procedure / 02	Quality Records
3	CORP / CMR / Procedure / 03	Internal Quality Audit
4	CORP / CMR / Procedure / 04	Non conformity control
5	CORP / CMR / Procedure / 05	Corrective Action
6	CORP / CMR / Procedure / 06	Preventive Action
7	CORP / CMR / Procedure / 07	Management Review

Accomplishments

This organization did not have any legal compliance when assessed at the start of the implementation. This was a dramatic turnaround in just nine months. Legal calendars and legal registers were created for each site, fulfilling each state's and the country's requirements. This led to an almost 100% legal compliance accomplishment. See Figure 8.4.

The company adopted a process approach from a strong functional approach. The departmental audit approach was changed to a process approach with IMS audit. This adoption of the process approach with process owners is helping transform the organization slowly.

A focus on management review and data-based decision making improved the organization significantly. In fact, the company has seen tremendous growth in the five years since the implementation of the integrated management system. This growth can be traced back to the streamlining of processes and increase in efficiency that is associated with integration and standardization.

The organization was document heavy. One of the benefits of the IMS was a dramatic reduction in documentation. Since the implementation, the organization has continued the standardization of processes. The current level of standardization for enterprise processes is 100% consistency within level II documents. The only site-specific procedures are the emergency preparedness and response, operational controls, and legal register documents.

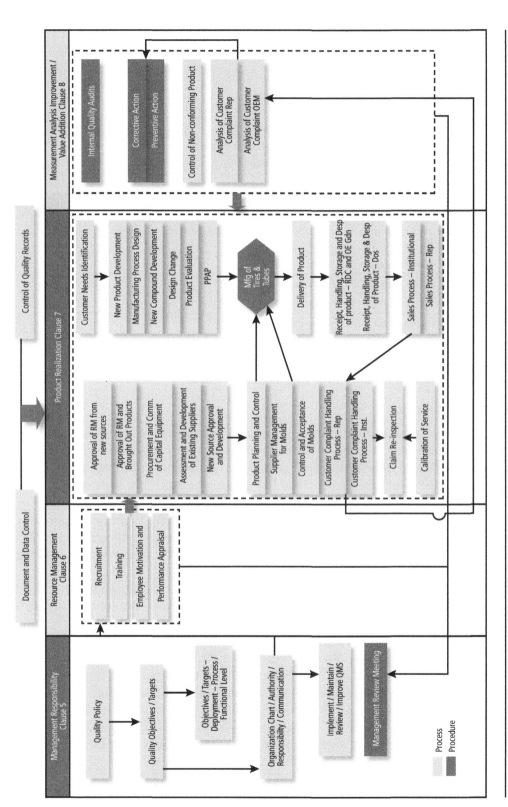

Figure 8.4 Business process cycle.

The design FMEAs, process FMEAs and E and HS risk analysis, which were started by the authors, were subsequently worked on by the organization with cross functional teams to reduce risk tremendously.

Omnex EwIMS Software

This organization also implemented Omnex APQP/PPAP management software for managing new product development launch and AQuA Pro for product and process risk management. AQuA Pro is being used in a few sites and it will become company-wide soon.

The new product development push came from top management and is used company-wide for standardizing product launch. The APQP/PPAP manager has a corporate process owner and an Asia-wide implementation.

9

Integration in a Service Environment—a Case Study

The authors implemented an integrated management system for a large construction start up in the Middle East. We developed a management system from the ground up as the site was being built. It was an integral part of the city and was in the construction phase when we started the implementation. It is what one would imagine a governmental program would be, and its purpose was to serve the people of the city. The scope of the implementation covered the construction phase, site personnel, and customers. Rather than document what they were doing, the management system documented what the processes should be. This is an example of a major implementation involving more than two thousand people in a service enterprise within a governmental agency.

The initiative began with an interview with the various functional groups of this government entity. An analysis of the quality, environmental, and health and safety system was made and a preliminary risk analysis was conducted. Based on the interview and assessment of the site functional departments, as well as the analysis conducted, relevant processes were identified. Because this was a very specific bid, there were clear stipulations on what one could and could not do. The set up was quite particular as per the quote and the authors had to strictly follow the Request for Proposal requirements.

The implementation was planned into four phases as illustrated in Table 9.1.

Table 9.1 Four-phase implementation plan.

Phase	Milestones	Target Date to End By
Phase 1	Analysis of the QEHS and a situational analysis	Month 1
	Interim Progress Report	Month 1
	Development of a Project Implementation Plan	Month 2
Phase 2	Development of Documentation – Levels I and II	Complete by Month 6
	Development of an Implementation Plan	Complete by Month 6
Phase 3	QEHS process training development	Develop by Month 8
	Pilot Training & Implementation	Month 9
	Overall Implementation	Completed by Month 12
Phase 4	Develop IT Solution for the QEHS	Completed by Month 12
Project Management	Phases I , II, III, and IV	Throughout Project

Developing the Documentation

Two related manuals were developed, a quality manual and a health and safety manual. Contents for both manuals were similar (see below), but the environmental health and safety manual focused on EMS and OHSAS conformance.

The manuals were well developed and professionally designed to include the company logo. The manuals have almost identical content, with only the policy statements differing. The organizational design included a director for QHSE and separate managers for quality and EHS. Although the two manuals presented substantially duplicate information, they were designed separately because of the contractual requirements of the RFP.

Quality Manual		HSE Manual	
1	Contents and Revision Status. 2	1	Contents and Revision Status. 2
2	Revision History 3	2	Revision History 3
3	Organization's Profile. 4-5	3	Introduction 4
4	Scope of Manual 6	4	Organization Profile 5-6
5	Business Process Map 7-8	5	Scope of Manual 7
6	Interaction Matrix. 9	6	Business Process Map 8-9
7	IMS Quality Policy. 10	7	Interaction Matrix. 10
8	Definitions 11	8	IMS HSE Policy 11
9	Organization Chart. 12	9	Definitions 12
10	Responsibility and Authority. 13-14	10	Organization Chart. 13
11	Management Representative 15	11	Responsibility and Authority. 14-15
		12	Management Representative 16

The business process map as demonstrated in the manual shows a completely integrated process map with processes as displayed in Figure 9.1. The process map shows no processes for product realization (7.0 in ISO 9001). What customers want in customer related processes and the shipping of the product to the customer is not detailed. The lack of processes can be explained by the fact that senior management was focused on documenting the site as-is in order to have it help them in their current state of construction.

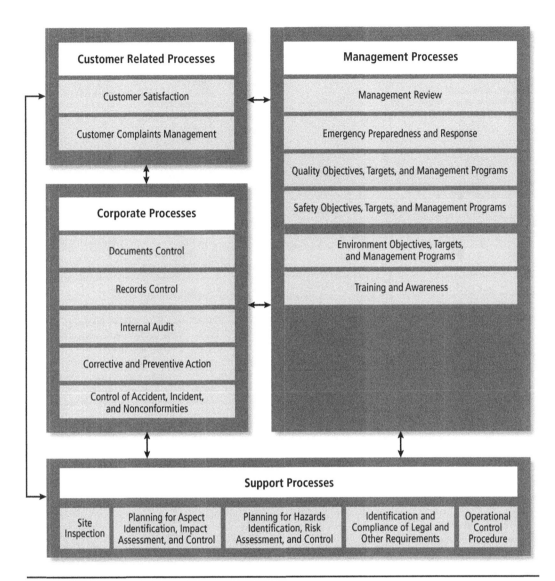

Figure 9.1 Business process map.

Level II Procedures

The Level II procedures were focused on the state of the business at the time of the construction. The processes could be grouped as project (construction) oriented processes and processes that focused on follow up to ensure actions by contractors were completed on time. All of design was represented by a design review that assessed construction/project related design. The processes documented were fairly generic (see Figure 9.2) and could have been designed for any organization.

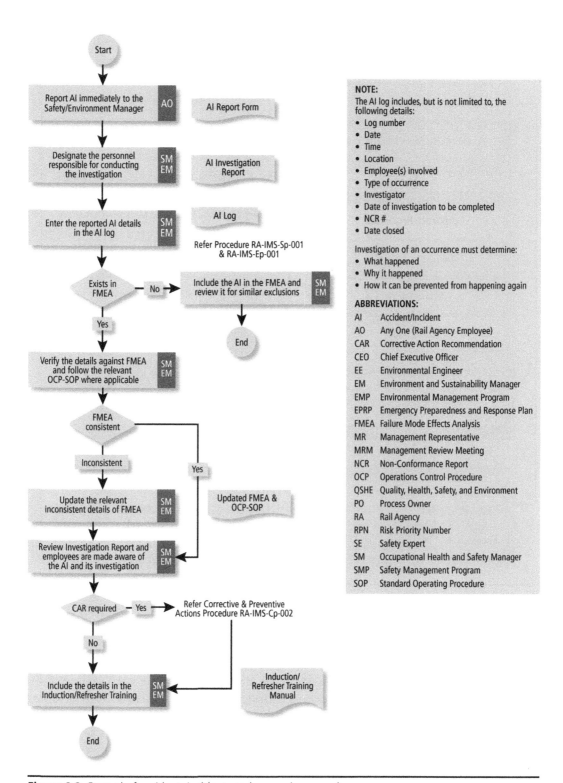

Figure 9.2 Control of accident, incident, and near-miss procedure.

It reflects the stage of the organization and the newness of the employees in their related jobs. This implementation suffered from a disconnect because senior management was not "hands on" with the system. Processes were for the most part designed by consultants.

Integrated Risk—QMS, EMS, and OHSAS

The FMEA and aspects/impacts/hazard methodology was used to document the quality, environmental, and health and safety risks of the organization. The risk analysis was divided and contracted with several consulting groups professing knowledge of quality, environmental, and health and safety risks. No site employees were involved in the risk assessment

The "site" under construction has little to no historical data as it relates to failures and their likelihood of occurrence. If the risk assessments were conducted with the current design and historical data in, then the team could have made significant improvements. In fact, if the company had flown the team to Thailand, conducted the risk analysis in Bangkok, and benchmarked a similar Thai site, much improvement could have resulted. If cooperation with the Thai site or another site had been possible (interviewing staff and also accessing quality, environmental and health and safety incident history), it would have been even better. This is the experience that could have been gained from a benchmarking exercise. Access to the failure history of an operating site would have been invaluable. Similarly, examining the controls being used would have helped the Middle East site in planning how to optimize their current controls.

QEHS Training Development and Implementation

The authors helped create training for each of the processes of the different functions affected. Training was conducted for those who had to be aware of the process and also for those who had to perform the processes. Two thousand employees and contractors were trained in just about four months.

The system went live at the end of 12 months and then was followed up by internal audits followed by third-party audits.

Current Situation: The site is in full swing, functioning effectively, and is very popular with the public. It is known for being safe, with high customer satisfaction. By the way, the quality system has been updated three times in the last five years.

10

Integration in an Aerospace Organization—a Case Study

Omnex has helped many different aerospace companies that engage in machining, electronics, fabrication and assembly to achieve AS9100 certification. The company discussed in this case study manufactures chemical products that are centered around materials supplied for electronic products. They have manufacturing plants worldwide including two facilities and an R&D center in the United States, one plant in Europe, and one plant in China. We will call this company Aerco.

Products manufactured by Aerco Corporation are actually produced from two main product lines. The commonality of products and processes was an important factor in developing design and process FMEAs for the organization to satisfy both AS9100 and ISO/TS 16949 (Automotive standard).

The company wanted to implement an integrated ISO/TS 16949 and AS9100 system from their current ISO 9001 QMS system. The scope of the initial implementation was the US plants and the R&D center. The project started with an initial assessment of the company. The assessment highlighted the following areas needing improvement (many nonconformances were summarized):

- Documented QMS system is based on the clauses of the standard, and consequently does not reflect the actual operational processes of the organization.

- QMS, as constituted, does not effectively align performance objectives with customer requirements and competitive necessity.

- Objectives are not deployed to different functions and levels in a way that supports development of performance and process metrics supporting achievement of high level objectives.

- Many methods of communication are employed; however, there are no defined processes for internal and/or external communication that would ensure an essential "shared level of understanding" throughout the organization.

- Information on the performance of the organization, its QMS processes, and its products is generally not communicated within the plants.

- Many requirements are missing in training and competency.

- Procedure 123 that allows sales to waive specified requirements is not allowed by ISO/TS 16949 or AS9100.
- Nothing prevents sales from accepting an order prior to passing a manufacturing feasibility review.
- FMEA and control plans are not used much in the organization. Existing FMEAs and control plans show lack of understanding.
- There is evidence of missing verification of job set ups.
- There is no preventive action process in the organization
- There is no evidence of monitoring of QMS non-manufacturing processes (for example, purchasing).
- None of the ISO/TS 16949 8.2.3 clauses are addressed to date (for example, process studies, maintaining capability established at Production Part Approval Process (PPAP)).
- First pass yield data are not responded to promptly.
- Operators can record actual data such as weight with no check for accuracy.
- There is evidence of gage R&R not being performed using the operators involved (for example, gold cell).
- Control plans are not implemented as required by ISO/TS 16949.
- Maintenance activities are not predictive. Records indicate that preventive maintenance is conducted on time.
- Maintenance schedule defaults to twice per year, which may not be adequate in some cases.
- Internal labs are missing a scope statement, measurement uncertainty is not known, and R&R studies are not completed.
- There are many issues in 7.6 and Management Systems Analysis (MSA) requirements.
- There are many issues with supplier management processes.
- No evidence exists of required information for the nonconforming material tags.

The company had many gaps when compared to ISO/TS 16949 and AS9100. However, after reviewing all the different case studies in this book, the reader will notice that gaps in the beginning do not hamper an integrated management systems implementation.

Typically at the end of an initial assessment, the authors will work with key decision makers to share the findings and to design the plan to implement the system. The implementation is generally more than just getting certification and this example was no different. The highlights of this implementation included:

a. Creating a process-focused process map.

b. Ensuring objectives are customer and strategy focused and ensuring that focus flows down in the entire company.

c. Teaching and implementing APQP and FMEA. Though this is a requirement of ISO/TS 16949 and AS9100 (risk management), it is also a quality improvement strategy when implemented with the correct focus and mindset.

d. Developing an integrated and standardized management system that can develop into a global system including integration of ISO 14001 at a later stage.

The authors, working with the client's quality and operational senior management, agreed to the following implementation plan as shown in Table 10.1.

Table 10.1 Implementation plan.

Time	Task	2013					2014			
		Aug	Sep	Oct	Nov.	Dec	Jan	Feb	Mar	Apr
13	Discovery Analysis	X								
2	Understanding TS/AS Implementation Team and Management Training		X							
5	APQP Training		X							
4	Documentation Workshop (2)		X							
2	Quality Manual / Process Map / BMS Control Plan									
6	Documentation Development			X	X		X			
1	Document Review				X					
3	Documentation Development				X		X	X		
4	FMEA / Design Verification Plan & Report (DVP&R) (Test Plans) / Control Plans Coaching			X	X		X			
2	Roll Out (Coaching for process owners to be audit-ready						X			
3	Internal Auditor Training							X		
3	Internal Audit (3 teams)							X		
3	Individual Consults as needed			X	X		X	X	X	X
Total: 51	Registrar Audit									X

One of the first tasks in the implementation was to develop a quality manual that would add value to the organization. As we mentioned in Chapter 7 in regard to Old Bakery, the quality manual requirements in both AS9100 and ISO/TS 16949 can be satisfied by a two-page manual; however, it would not be as valuable as the manual outlined below. It was the goal of the Omnex team to create a manual that would function as a marketing tool for the organization. See Figure 10.1.

An important ingredient of the manual is a process map. For Aerco, the process map had to represent the entire entity including corporate, R&D, and the two manufacturing sites. In very large companies there can be two process maps, a corporate process map laying out the standardized corporate global processes and a site process map showing the global and site processes. In this case, the authors developed one process map for the organization as shown in Figure 10.2. The process map shows 46 processes company wide. See Table 10.2.

The authors identified the process owners and scheduled two-day documentation development workshops to facilitate groups of process owners and teams in developing documentation. The authors used a well-developed process to develop and document a level II document. See the format that the authors use in Figure 10.3.

Introduction to Aerco Corporation

    I. Vision and Mission Statement

    II. Aerco Organizational Chart

    III. Quality Policy

    IV. Environmental Policy

    V. Scope of the ISO/TS 16949:2009, AS9100C, and
       ISO 9001:2008 Implementation

    VI. Products – Aerco

    VII. Process Map – Aerco

    VIII. Process List

    IX. BMS Control Plan

    X. Description of the BMS

    XI. Clause-Procedure Cross Walk

Figure 10.1 Aerco quality manual contents.

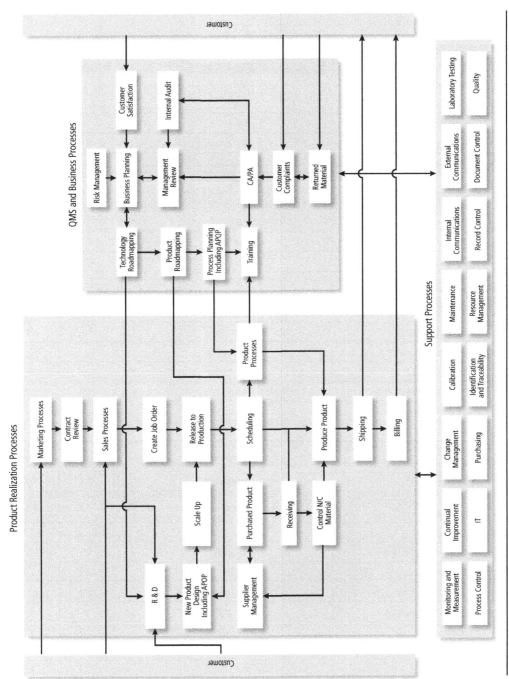

Figure 10.2 Process map developed.

Table 10.2 Level II procedures.

Process Number	Process Name	Related Aerco Documents	Process Owner	Principal Locations	AS Clause	TS Clause
	Risk Management		TBD		7.1.2	
	Customer Satisfaction		Sales		5.2; 8.2.1	5.2; 8.2.1
	Sales Processes		Sales		NA	NA
	Business Planning		HQ Services		5.4	5.4
	Marketing		Sales		NA	NA
	Contract Review		Sales		7.2.1; 7.2.2	7.2.1; 7.2.2
	Technology Road Mapping		R & D		5.4	5.4
	Product Road Mapping		R & D		5.4	5.4
	Process Planning/APQP		Operations		7.1	7.1
	R & D Processes		R & D		NA	NA
	New Product Design/APQP		R & D		7.1; 7.3	7.1; 7.3
	Scale Up		Manufacturing Engineering		7.5.2	7.5.2
	Job Order Creation		Operations		NA	NA
	Production Release		Operations		7.5.1	7.5.1
	Scheduling		Operations		7.5.1	7.5.1
	Purchasing Processes		Finance		7.4	7.4
	Supplier Management		Purchasing		7.4	7.4
	Receiving		Operations		7.4.3	7.4.3
	Production Process Implementation		Operations		7.5.2	7.5.2
	Product Production		Operations		7.5	7.5
	Control of Non-conforming Material		Operations		8.3	8.3
	Training		HR		6.2.2	6.2.2
	Management Review		President		5.6	5.6
	Internal Auditing		Quality		8.2.2	8.2.2
	Corrective and Preventive Action		Operations		8.5	8.5
	Resource Management		Operations		6	6
	Shipping		Operations		7.5.5	7.5.5
	Document Control		Quality		4.2	4.2
	Record Control		IT		4.2.4	4.2.4
	IT Processes		HQ Services		6.3; 6.4	6.3; 6.4
	Monitoring and Measurement		Operations		8	8
	Process Control		Operations		7.5	7.5
	Billing		Finance		NA	NA

(Continued)

Table 10.2 Level II procedures. *(Continued)*

Process Number	Process Name	Related Aerco Documents	Process Owner	Principal Locations	AS Clause	TS Clause
	Customer Complaints		Sales		8.2.1	8.2.1
	Returned Material		Quality		8.3; 8.5.2	8.3; 8.5.2
	Continual Improvement		Operations		8.5	8.5
	Change Management		R & D		7.3.7	7.1.4; 7.3.7
	Calibration		Quality		7.6	7.6
	Identification and Traceability		Operations		7.5.3	7.5.3
	Maintenance		Operations		7.1; 7.2.1	7.2.1; 7.5.1.4; 7.5.1.5
	Internal Communications		President		5.5.3	5.5.3
	External Communications		Sales		7.2.3	7.2.3
	Laboratory Testing		Quality		7.6	7.6.3
	Quality Processes		Operations			

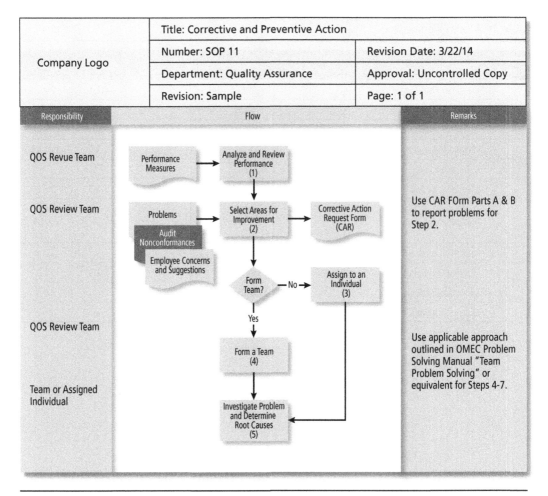

Figure 10.3 Recommended format for level II.

The documentation was completed and the doc review conducted. This was followed by a roll out of the documentation. Again, there was a strict, well defined process where the process owners rolled out the documentation and conducted their own training. Subsequently, the implementation officially started and records were collected.

This implementation is currently well underway and this company is awaiting certification. One of the problems the authors experienced while conducting this implementation was a lack of top management involvement. This lack of involvement means that the implementation is very much led by the quality function and as such may not reach its full potential for improvement.

11

Integration in a Semiconductor Organization—a Case Study

A fabless semiconductor* organization (we'll call it Asia Semi) requested Omnex to support it in achieving ISO/TS 16949 and ISO 14001 certification. This was a requirement to satisfy a customer that mandated certification to both standards. There was a great sense of urgency because this company had approached their registrar for an audit and it had failed in two major areas—lack of process approach, and no APQP or core tool utilization.

It is always the human dynamic that drives an implementation. In this case, it was the solid quality manager and a high-strung quality director who played into the picture. Another key player was a program manager who piloted the first APQP and FMEA based product and an operations director who helped the implementation in their overseas location.

The company was managed by overseas managers who did not enter into the picture much, and who for the most part worked with the quality manager who spoke the same language. Communications on the implementation usually went from the quality manager to the senior managers of the organization. They had hired experts to help them and they followed the process as it was laid out.

There were several difficulties in this implementation: limited time for process development and implementation, little involvement with foreign locations, and a lack of understanding of APQP and core tools company-wide.

– *Fabless semiconductor organizations cannot be certified to ISO/TS 16949 since ISO/TS 16949 certification requires manufacturing. However, the organization found a registrar willing to give them a certificate.*

Organization of the Company

There were four locations included in the scope of the implementation. Most of the staff were located in the United States and in Asia Location 1. The implementation focused much attention on the U.S., Asia Location 1, and Asia Location 2 (see Tables 11.1 and 11.2).

Table 11.1 USA and Asia 1 implementation.

USA	Asia Location 1
Document Control	Customer Communication (FAE/Sales)
Management Responsibilities	HR
Human Resources – Employee Training & Competency	Customer Satisfaction
MRD (Contract Review and Finalization)	Order Administration
Product Design and Development	Supplier Evaluation and Qualification
Operations (Product Engineering)	Analysis/Reliability Testing
Purchasing	Subcontractor Monitoring and Audits
Quote	Customer Audits
QA (RMA/FA/CAR/Calibration)	Internal Audits
Labs	Product Realization Testing
	Product Engineering
	Purchasing
	Returned Materials
	Quality Assurance
	Warehousing

Table 11.2 Asia 2 and 3 implementation.

Asia Location 2	Asia Location 3
Customer Communication (FAE/Sales)	Product Design and Layout
Product Design	Labs
Internal Audits	
Supplier Evaluation and Qualification	
Subcontractor Monitoring and Audits	
QA (RMA/FA/Calibration)	
Labs	

Documentation Development

Documentation development focused the Level I manual and Level II processes. Omnex consultants conducted workshops to develop the Level II processes. The authors also worked with the organization to edit and improve many documents that were close to conformance with the standard. We met little to no resistance in documentation development and the organization accepted all suggestions for ensuring the documents met the requirements of the standard.

The document review was conducted and the organization fixed all the issues found.

See Level I manual (Figure 11.1), integrated process maps (Figure 11.2), and Level II documentation list (Table 11.3). The process map and the one for Old Bakery in Chapter 7 are good examples of process maps. Both of these process maps don't show any of the problems of functional orientation or clause orientation, the two failure modes of process maps.

The current quality manual has undergone many iterations and style changes in the last ten years through many different implementations. This manual is missing one element that the authors believe is an important part of any quality manual (that is, the BMS control plan). An example of this was provided in Chapter 6 of *How an Integrated and Standardized Management System Performs for Maximum Effectiveness*. It is reproduced in Figure 11.3.

In Figure 11.1, the organization chose to have separate quality and environmental policies instead of integrating them. Integration should not be done thoughtlessly, but with reason. The authors believe it is good to have senior management communicate their quality and environmental policies in different statements so that the message is clear and unambiguous. Aerco product design and the organizational focus toward using less power was a good fit toward positive environmental impact.

Introduction to Asia Semi

   I. Vision and Mission Statement

   II. Asia Semi Organizational Chart

   III. Quality Policy

   IV. Environmental Policy

   V. Scope of the ISO/TS 16949:2009 and ISO 14001:2004 Implementation

   VI. Products – Asia Semi

   VII. Process Map – Asia Semi

   VIII. Process List

   IX. Description of the Management System and the Main Elements of the Environmental Management System

Figure 11.1 ISO/TS 16949 and ISO 14001 Manual (Level I).

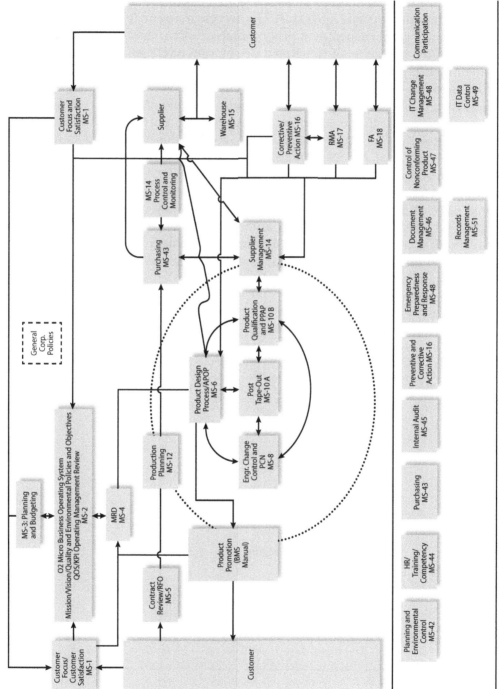

Figure 11.2 Process map.

Table 11.3 Development of level II procedures.

Process Number	Process Name	Current Asia Semi Procedure(s)	Process Owner	Principal Locations
NA	Mission, Vision, Policy, and Environmental Mission		Removed for Confidentiality	
MS-1	Customer Focus and Customer Satisfaction			
MS-2	Business Operating System and Continual Improvement			
MS-3	Business Planning and Budgeting			
MS-4	MRD			
MS-5	Contract Review			
MS-6	Product Design Process/APQP			
MS-8	Engineering Change Control and PCN			
	Product Promotion			
MS-10A and B	A: Post Tape Out			
	B: Product Qualification and PPAP			
MS-12	Production Planning			
MS-14	Supplier Management			
MS-15	Warehouse			
MS-16	Corrective and Preventive Action including 8-D			
MS-17	RMA			
MS-18	FA			
MS-41	Emergency Preparedness and Response			
MS-42	Planning and Environmental Controls			
MS-43	Purchasing			
MS-44	HR/Training/Competency			
MS-45	Internal Audit (Product, Process and System and Compliance)			
MS-46	Document Management			
MS-47	Nonconforming Product			
MS-48	IT Change Management			
MS-49	IT Data Control and Security			
MS-50	Communication, Participation, and Consultation			
MS-51	Record Management			

Process Activity	Customer Req/ Expectation	Key Process/ COP	Measurement	Responsibility	Acceptance Criteria 2014 Q1, Q2, Q3, Q4		Review Frequency	Control Methods	Comments/ Reaction
				EXAMPLES					
Business Fulfillment	On-time delivery	K	% on-time in operations	Logistics	94, 95, 96, 96%		4/yr	Monthly management meeting	Corrective action after 3 consecutive
			% on-time to customer	Production control	100%		4/yr	Trend chart	C/A is more than 15% off target
Customer Complaint	Provide timely response	C	Complaint response	Quality	10 days		4/Yr	Production control dept	Continue to monitor
Design & Development	Meet timing requirement		Time to market	Design/dev	52 weeks		Weekly	Quality department	R, Y, G reaction
Business Creation	Innovation		Patents filed	Design	20 per year		Monthly	Design meeting	Continue to monitor

Business Management System Control Plan

Organization: _____

General Manager: _____

Product Description: _____

Issue/Rev Date: _____

Figure 11.3 Business management system control plan.

The organization conducted quality risk analysis using DFMEAs. Being fabless (that is, no manufacturing of wafers), it did not do PFMEA. Environmental risk is assessed throughout all of the organization in its processes, labs, and the product itself. Both environmental FMEAs (EFMEA) and design FMEAs were new to this organization. We worked closely with teams to create the documentation and understand the risks. This organization faced one problem in this implementation. Although it used the EFMEA, the organization did not quantify severity, occurrence, or detection numbers and this became an issue during the audit.

About 30% of the level II documents (about 30 processes in this organization) are assigned to global process owners outside of the US.

Roll Out and Initial Audit

The documentation was rolled out throughout the organization by the process owners. However, process owners and site employees did not really understand what it meant to follow a process and to collect records as required. The initial audit conducted showed the overall weaknesses in the implementation. Each location was audited and received no less than 50 to 60 nonconformances. The assessment was an eye opener in terms of what was required by the standard to show fully implemented processes.

Third-party Audit

The organization fixed its nonconformances and conducted a second internal audit. After the second audit and subsequent corrective actions, the company passed the third-party audit without difficulty. As mentioned earlier, the issue of not rating risk for environmental issues came up, as did the internal audit checklist and the notes in a turtle diagram for the internal audit. This brings up the issue of conformance audits versus performance audits. ISO/TS 16949 and AS9100 now are encouraging performance audits. In ISO/TS 16949, it is called prioritizing the audit and the focus is on whether an audit is performing or not. In AS9100 they are using a PEAR, or Process Effectiveness Assessment Report, to gage processes.

When a complex QMS or EMS is initially implemented, the auditor should use a checklist to ensure that the system is being followed and not whether the system is effective. System effectiveness comes after the system is mature. These are some of the complicated issues not considered by the writers of the ISO/TS 16949 or AS9100 for new organizations adopting their standards.

12

Software Enabled Integrated Management System for the Enterprise

Enterprise integrated management systems software enables enterprise processes company wide. In fact, without software, it would be quite difficult to implement integrated management systems in large organizations. In other words it is difficult to get both integration and standardization that cuts across design, manufacturing, sales, and warehouse sites in multiple countries and languages. Omnex often calls it the challenge of the enterprise—multiple sites, in multiple countries, using multiple languages and recognizing multiple cultures. See Figure 12.1.

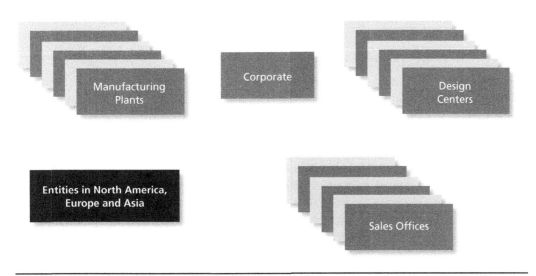

Figure 12.1 The challenge of enterprise: Multi-site, multi-language, and multi-cultural.
Copyright 2012. Omnex. All rights reserved.

Software enabled integrated management systems are designed to solve this problem and provide integration and standardization in an enterprise. What are the characteristics of a software-enabled integrated management system? They are:

- Enterprise-wide Web-based system
- Manage multiple sites
- Support multiple languages and multiple date conventions
- Integrated with Email notification, reminders, and escalation services
- Ready to integrate with legacy and ERP systems
- One-point user authentication
- Role-based security
- Fully integrated solutions; Lean data entry
- Includes enterprise integrated processes
- Includes, at a minimum, functionality of ISO 9001, ISO 14001, ISO 45001, and FSSC 22000
- Ability to add one site or management system and then scale up

Read more about each of these characteristics in the next section.

Enterprise-Wide Web-Based System

The software should be available to all users in the enterprise, including employees, suppliers, and customers. Using a browser, anyone with an email ID and a password should be able to come into the system. Employee access seems self-explanatory. How about suppliers and customers? Suppliers need access to documentation that affects them. They need to be able to provide documents for new product development in terms of PPAP or FAI and they need to be able to do problem solving and corrective action. Suppliers are rated, they provide KPI information, and they are audited. In fact, suppliers are a key part of the enterprise.

Similarly, customers need to interact with the organization. They need to access relevant documents, review PPAP or FAI information, receive corrective action reports, audit the organization, and so on.

Any enterprise software system needs to be able to provide access to employees, suppliers, and customers and have functionality to handle their specific needs.

Manage Multiple Sites

The software should be able to model the entire enterprise with each of the sites and should understand the concept of *entity*. Entity is the organizational hierarchy that describes which site or organizational entity reports to another. Each of the modules should be able to take advantage of site and entity design. See Figure 12.1 for sites.

When you choose a site in the in the Document Manager drop down, it will show you the document structure of that site. When you click on the folder, the table of contents will show. How does the entity structure come into play? It comes into play when we ask for reports for Americas, for example, or for Europe. Data then gets aggregated from the Divisions and Sites in Americas and/or Europe. For example, how many documents were changed in Europe? How many new documents in each region? In this way, both site and entity concepts come into play.

The auditing module should be able to show the audits in each site by simply selecting the drop down of the site. If a user has the rights to view that site, then the audit calendar of that site should be displayed. The division should be a site in the software as well. When Division is chosen, then the audit list for Division is shown in the calendar. This includes each of the sites reporting to the Division. In this fashion the site and entity concepts work together.

Support Multiple Languages and Multiple Date Conventions

Enterprise integrated management systems must be able to support English, Spanish, Chinese, German, French, and Japanese. The menu should automatically change to accommodate users from the various countries. The software must go further and provide for the ability for translation depending on the functionality.

Language is important, but sometimes date conventions do not communicate. In the United States, the convention for displaying dates is Month/Date/Year. In some countries the order is Date/Month/Year. You can imagine a date of 1/11/2014 could mean January 11 or November 1, depending where you are in the world.

The software should be able to capture the different holidays in countries. This feature is used when planning resources for product launches and/or in preventive maintenance planning.

Integrated Email Notification, Reminders, and Escalation Services

This is an important function of enterprise integrated management systems software. Email notifications are an important tool to inform personnel of actions to take in relationship to the system. There are multiple actions that need to be performed in each of the processes in an integrated management system, from auditing to document control. Well-designed software will notify the person responsible and then remind them a preset number of times. After the limit is reached, it will notify either the next level of management or the person designated in the notification route for escalation purposes.

Ready to Integrate with Legacy and ERP Systems

Integrated management systems software focuses on processes and documentation for management systems. To function effectively the software must integrate with ERP, HR, and other legacy software. Ease of integration with other packages is a must.

One-Point User Authentication

Users in organizations are tired of having to remember multiple IDs and passwords. Enterprise integrated management systems must adopt methodology like Active Directory so that users do not have multiple sign-ons to the system.

Role-Based Security

Role-based security permits selected access to folders and documents in various workflows. In the Document Manager, only authorized documents or levels of documents may be viewed. In product- and process-based modules such as risk manager or new product development, access is permitted by product and process. Access could be further restricted to the level of task or document. Access and viewing rights could even go to the level of drop down lists in a software. Role-based security and the ability to fine tune access based on organizational requirements is essential.

Fully Integrated Solutions; Lean Data Entry

Lean data entry goes hand and hand with the linkages between the various workflows. Lean data entry focuses on one aspect of the linkages, non-redundant data entry. Gages appear in the control plan and also in the calibration software. Machines and production lines are set up in the preventive maintenance software and the same fields are used for conducting process FMEAs and control plans. Users, products, and processes appear again and again in each work flow. A fully integrated system will allow each workflow or module to talk to the others. There is more about linkages later in this chapter.

Includes Enterprise Integrated Processes

We have defined an integrated enterprise process earlier in this chapter. A system is made up of interrelated integrated enterprise processes all having these characteristics: a) It is accessible to anyone in the enterprise either inside or outside the company; b) The process owner has the ability to manage the process, to measure, monitor, and improve it; c) It is a key process of a management system; and d) It is linked to other key processes as required. Since an integrated enterprise management system is made up of integrated processes, it indirectly has the same characteristics. This is explained in greater detail later in this chapter.

Includes Minimum Functionality of ISO 9001, ISO 14001, ISO 45001, and FSSC 22000

At a minimum it satisfies the functionalities of QMS, EMS, OHSMS, and FSMS (see Figure 12.2). The integration of management systems arises from common requirements and expectations in each of the management systems. This leads to a common list of web-enabled processes that can help implement integration and standardization in an enterprise.

Enterprise Integrated Management Systems	
a. Risk Management	o. New Product Development Processes
b. Sales and Contract Review	
c. New Product Introduction	p. Product and Process Risk Management using FMEAs
d. Product and Process Risk	
e. Training, Competency, and Benefits	q. Manage the Change Process (product and process change)
f. Continual Improvement Programs (Performance Management)	r. First Article or PPAP
g. Internal, Supplier, and Third-party Audit Management	s. Requirements Gathering to fulfillment (Sales and Contract Review)
h. Document Control and Distribution	t. Manufacturing Process Control including SPC
i. Record Control	
j. Risk Management	u. Measurement System Analysis including MSA
k. Performance Management KPIs and Process Measurable measurement and monitoring	v. Internal, supplier and 3rd party audit management
l. Management Review and Continual Improvement	w. Investigation and Corrective Action
m. Training, Competency, and Benefits	x. Continual Improvement Programs (Performance Management)
n. Preventive and Breakdown Maintenance	

Note: Scheduling to Delivery, Direct Purchasing and Customer Satisfaction were purposely left out of the list above since those are accomplished via ERP software or other specialized software.

Figure 12.2 Enterprise integrated management processes.

Ability to Add One Site or Management System and Then Scale Up

It lets an organization easily add management systems one at a time without too much complication.

Enterprise integrated management system software should work the same way for QMS, EMS, OHSMS, and FSMS. Let us examine a concrete example of corrective actions. If the corrective action system initially is implemented for external quality problems or issues (that is, from customers), the same module should work for internal quality and supplier quality problems or issues as well. It should be as simple as choosing a different field in a drop down. Of course, fields and notifications selected can change, so the software must be able to easily adapt between customer issues, internal issues, and supplier issues. The same software modules should, by choosing environmental (external), allow the user to use the same functionality to implement corrective action for EMS. The fields will change and different information will be gathered about the external environmental compliant, and different people in the organization will be notified. Enterprise integrated management systems will be designed in such a manner that QMS, EMS, OHSMS, and FSMS can be implemented by the organization sequentially. Integrated management system software and workflow should be designed to work in one site or one management system and then scaled up. This should be the case for all of the workflows in Figure 12.2.

ENTERPRISE INTEGRATED PROCESSES

This section will identify five characteristics of enterprise integrated processes:

- Provides accessibility inside and outside of the enterprise
- Satisfies requirements of QMS, EMS, OHSMS, and FSMS standards
- Allows the organization to measure, monitor, and improve the process
- Is a corporate or site process
- Allows linkages that promote efficiency and effectiveness

Provides Accessibility Inside and Outside the Enterprise

The software should be accessible to anyone anywhere (via security)—employees, contractors, suppliers, or customers. In fact, the general public should be able to access documents deemed necessary by the organization.

Satisfies Requirements of QMS, EMS, OHSMS, and FSMS Standards

Integrated enterprise processes enforce standardization and integration: Standardization, the same process company wide. Integration, all the requirements or "shalls" of QMS, EMS, OHSMS, and FSMS in its implementation.

By definition, the enterprise processes have to satisfy the "shalls" of the different standards. The design should be seamless in how they are able to add QMS, EMS, OHSMS, or FSMS sequentially. When standards are added for approval, the management, and the sign offs in each process, need to be unique to the standard if required by the organization. In fact, independent or non-integrated management of processes could be the starting point for integration.

Allows the Organization to Measure, Monitor, and Improve the Process

A process owner has the ability to manage the process, to measure, monitor, and improve.

Each of the enterprise processes will have its own process measurements. The process owner should be able to manage a process aggregated for the enterprise, each site, standard, product, process, or other variable. The software should allow a process improvement team to meet around a process and improve it.

Is a Corporate or Site Process

An integrated enterprise process is an enterprise or site process of a management system.

At a minimum, enterprise integrated management systems should satisfy the enterprise processes listed below. Optimally, it should include all the processes in Figure 12.2.

Allows Linkages That Promote Efficiency And Effectiveness

The management systems in an organization are inherently linked. For example, these are linkages between goals and objectives, KPIs, business reviews, and continual improvements. The linkages and the process area is called Performance Management in this book. The next area of linkages covered in this chapter is Risk Management. Linkages between processes allows one process to update the next or for several processes to be updated simultaneously. Many large and small enterprises complain about the lack of connectivity of processes or how one is updated and the others are not, or how one process is supposed to trigger another. Inherently, EwIMS systems need to design the multiple linkages between the processes and execute these processes via software for the effectiveness and efficiency of the enterprise.

Let us look at the linkages between the first two processes in our list.

Performance Management

Figure 12.3 shows that objectives set should be customer focused and result in measurables that are aligned and linked to business objectives. Key processes support the result measurables, which in turn are measured using process measurables. When process measurables improve, the company is able to meet its results or KPIs. This, in turn, helps the company meet objectives and satisfy customers.

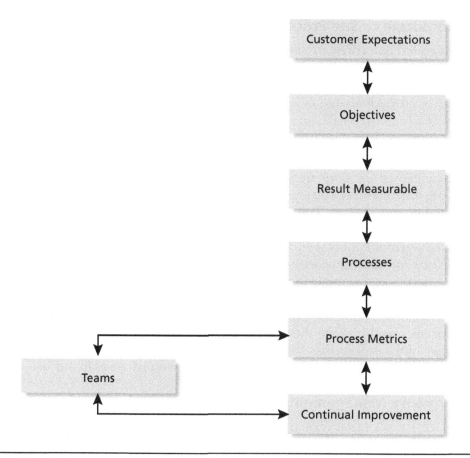

Figure 12.3 Aligning customer expectations, objectives, and result measureables.

A second set of linkages is shown in Figure 12.4, illustrating that Figure 12.3, performance management, and departmental and employee objectives and appraisals, are linked. The site objectives are deployed to the departments, which are then deployed to personnel. The idea is to make it a part of employee appraisals. In this way, overall objectives are tied to employee objectives. This is a good example of linkages that make processes effective.

Risk Management

Linkages between risk management, new product introduction, and change management are shown in Figure 12.5. The actual implementation includes a product and process validation process often called production part approval process or first article inspection.

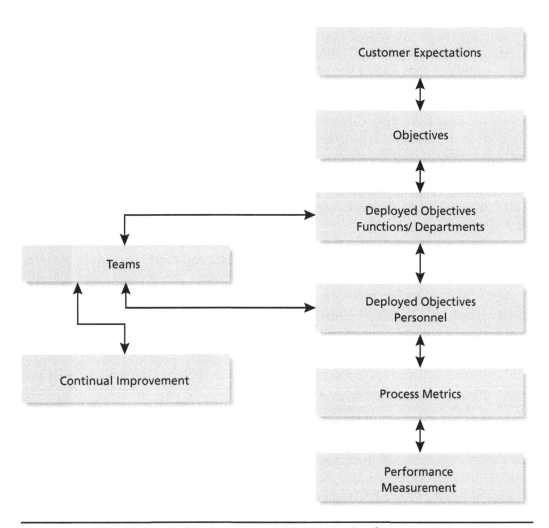

Figure 12.4 Linkages between objectives, personal objectives, and performance measurement.

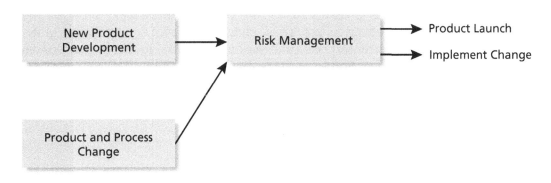

Figure 12.5 Linkages between risk management, new product introduction, and change management.

An enterprise integrated management process should allow the organization to seamlessly implement all the processes identified in Figure 12.1. The system has a workflow that allows the process owner to provide oversight of the process to measure, monitor, and improve its function. At the same time, it can allow site process owners ability to oversee the local site processes. In some cases, the enterprise may have three different managers in a site (for example, the QMS audit, the EMS audit, and the OHSAS audit). In this case, though the process is integrated and standardized, top management did not make organizational changes and have the integrated audit placed under one manager. It is very possible for a system to be integrated and management take the necessary steps for organizational alignment. The software should allow all combinations of audits by processes, enterprise, site, and standard.

Enterprise processes with the accessibility inside and outside of the enterprise, satisfying the requirements of QMS, EMS, OHSMS, and FSMS standards, allowing the organization to measure, monitor and improve the process, and allowing linkages that promote efficiency and effectiveness—these are the basic building blocks of the enterprise integrated management system.

SUMMARY

The enterprise integrated management software system has the ten characteristics described in the beginning of this chapter: Enterprise-wide Web-based functionality; ability to manage multiple sites; support for multiple languages and multiple date conventions; integrated Email notification, reminders, and escalation services; ready to integrate with legacy and ERP systems; one-point user authentication; role-based security; fully integrated solutions with Lean data entry; includes enterprise integrated processes; includes minimum functionality of ISO 9001, ISO 14001, ISO 45001, and FSSC 22000; and has the ability to add one site or management system and then scale up.

The building blocks of enterprise integrated software are the enterprise processes, which in turn are made up of five characteristics—accessibility inside and outside of the enterprise; ability to satisfy requirements of QMS, EMS, OHSMS, and FSMS standards; allows the organization to measure, monitor and improve the process; functions as a corporate or site process; and allows linkages that promote efficiency and effectiveness. These characteristics of enterprise integrated software and each of the enterprise processes are essential to the overall success of an IMS implementation. Software that satisfies the criteria in this chapter will allow a seamless and painless implementation. Any software that portrays itself as integrated management system software should meet the minimum requirements outlined in this chapter.

13

Lessons Learned from Integrated Management Systems Implementations

In this book we cover five implementations in the United States, Asia, and Arab countries—Old Bakery, Auto Tier One, the Middle East site, Aerco, and Asia Semi. These implementations prove, among other things, that integrated management systems can be implemented globally in many different cultures. We have implemented integrated management systems combining business excellence (this company used the European Quality Award criteria) and QMS as well as integration involving QMS, EMS, OHSMS, and social responsibility (EICC) standards in Europe. Most definitely, IMS works globally, not just in different cultures, but also in many different industries. Integrated management systems are a definite strategy in the food industry and the only way to really ensure food safety, high quality, and minimized environmental and health and safety risks. At a minimum, food companies should integrate food and quality management systems. As we have always said, when you implement FSMS, the quality management system comes for free since the requirements of ISO 9001 and FSSC 22000 have much in common. Large Europe-based food companies are implementing QMS, EMS, OHSMS, and FSMS. The other interesting implementation is the Middle East site, where a $300 million construction project implemented an integrated QMS, EMS, OHSMS during the construction phase. Arab countries have some of the most forward thinking companies in our experience. They seem to adopt the most current ideas through their use of consulting companies and advisors. The other interesting implementation is Aerco. The aerospace industry has large OEMs and large prime vendors. Prime vendors have implemented AS9100, but are slow to implement ISO 14001 or ISO 45001. The aerospace industry is rapidly modernizing and adopting many of the latest methodologies emerging from other industries. Integrated management systems may be another strategy for them to implement.

What are the commonalities in these implementations, what are the models that can be reused, and what are the lessons learned? The analysis can be done from the viewpoint of the following:

1. Top management mind set and involvement in the integration

2. Scoping the implementation

3. Improvement versus documentation

4. Level I manual

5. Processes/procedures

6. Audits

7. Process owners

8. Registration

TOP MANAGEMENT MINDSET AND INVOLVEMENT IN THE INTEGRATION

Of the five integrated management systems implementations featured in this book, the one with the greatest management involvement was Old Bakery. At Old Bakery, the authors worked with the management team to implement a customer-focused key measurables system. The greatest benefit management found in the implementation was with the linkage of customer expectations, objectives, and key measurables and improvement in the quality operating system. Top management in Old Bakery had begun to see positive improvement after just a few monthly management reviews that helped with their overall improvement and enthusiasm for the integrated management systems. This arrangement continues to thrive and the system has been extended to their other factories and sites.

Another implementation with heavy management involvement occurred at Automotive Tier One. This organization, as do many large automotive organizations in Asia, had two tiers of top management—executive management and corporate top management. The authors worked with top management and provided them with several days of coaching in integrated management systems. This set the stage for continuing good will in the months of implementation. This training was carried out to the plants, where top plant managers were trained. There was tremendous support by top management in the plant for the implementation. The support of corporate top management and plant management helped make this implementation a huge success. Then there is no wonder that this tier one has blazed new trails in the recent years making several acquisitions and expanding beyond their borders in Asia. The management system has also improved considerably since its implementation.

The other three implementations—the Middle East site, Aerco, and Asia Semi— had little to no management involvement. Each of these implementations suffered from this lack of management involvement. In two of them, a quality department led the effort and top management's goal was certification. The leadership and the push for implementation and certification came from the authors, rather than from company management. The real issue for these organizations would be the long-term success of their management systems, post involvement of the authors.

For long-term sustainability, a management system must transition from consultant led to top management led. For that to happen, it is important to coach top management during implementation so they understand the system and also during management review to ensure effective customer satisfaction, customer corrective action, and internal, customer and third-party audits. Management should understand that they have the responsibility and the authority to drive improvements. In Old Bakery and Auto Tier One, top management was using the management reviews to drive improvement. In the other three, they were conducting reviews to become registered or to keep the registration.

In the Middle East site, all the work was performed by lower levels of management; top management, to a large degree, were figureheads in the management system. In Asia Semi, management's entire goal was to achieve certification and not for the system to derive benefit. They were a purely product-oriented business that had little understanding of or respect for management systems or a disciplined way to operate. In Aerco, there was not enough interest from senior management in the management system.

Typically, an implementation is six to nine months long and has three phases. phase I—Management System Findings, Process Map and Quality Manual; phase II—Documentation Development; and phase III—System Implementation and Management Review. The implementation should interact with senior management in each of the phases. Here are some suggestions for successful implementation:

Phase I

- Interaction 1—Presentation on findings and implementation plan
- Interaction 2—Executive overview on integrated management systems
- Interaction 3—Review of process map, policies, and the manual

Phase II

- Interaction 4—Top management is involved as a team member or leader for a few top management processes. Review of management processes as they are developed.

Phase III

- Interaction 5—Top management is audited
- Interaction 6—Top management is coached on questions to ask during management review

At the very least top management should be coached on expectations of a management review and the expectations for top management during an audit.

SCOPING THE IMPLEMENTATION

The authors have always used integrated management systems when there are multiple management systems, multiple sites, and a short time for implementation. Here are the options in implementations:

a. Implement standardized and integrated processes in all sites for all management systems

b. Implement a standardized system in QMS in all sites and then add other management systems

c. Implement an integrated management system in one site and then add other sites

d. Implement an integrated management system in a few key processes in all sites

In the implementations discussed in this book, Auto Tier One and Asia Semi are examples of integration and standardization in all sites in all management systems. Old Bakery is an example of an integrated system in one site and the addition of other sites. Aerco is an implementation of two QMS systems in three sites (but not all sites). The Middle East site is an example of an integrated management system in one site. So what about the scope, why is it important?

The quality of the processes implemented is important. In this regard, option A, where integrated management systems are implemented in all sites, tends to be the implementations where the processes are the least effective. It is not possible to implement 30 to 50 processes as a best in class implementation. This same scenario applies to option C as well, where integrated management systems are applied to one site. The burden of designing and implementing 30 to 50 processes in a matter of months renders options A and C not the best scoping decisions. However, option A is the best choice if someone is interested in implementing multiple management systems globally in a short period of time. In this scenario, the company should choose a few processes to target as best in class with the remaining targeted for conformance. This is typically an organization with a deadline imposed by a customer or another external body.

Option B entails implementing 30 to 50 processes in one management system simultaneously in multiple sites. This option is same as option A, but it does not have the benefit of implementing all the management systems. Option A is superior to option B. Option A takes more effort, but the payback and value are much more.

So this leaves option D, the current favorite. This option is only possible if there is no time deadline imposed by external parties. In this scenario, each site can continue operating in QMS, EMS, and OHSMS without integration and standardization. The organization can phase in integration and standardization in stages, in each stage targeting BIC class processes. This will give the organization the ability to focus on key processes and derive the biggest benefit from them. Implementing best in class processes will be the topic of book three of the integrated management system series.

IMPROVEMENT VERSUS DOCUMENTATION

This is an important issue for top management and a message the authors try to communicate during the executive overview. Top management only achieves what they target. If they target certification, that is what they get. If they target improvement and certification, they will get that also. The organizations that targeted improvement included Auto Tier One. They got improvement, but not to the degree possible, due to the scoping of the processes (that is, they tried to do too much at once).

Old Bakery had the most improvement. For many reasons this implementation was the one most like option D. Even though we documented over 40 processes, the focus was on implementing a performance management system, phased new product development process with gates, and problem solving processes.

The other three systems, to a large degree, had certification as the primary objective. However, the organizations still enjoyed savings in implementation and maintenance, even though they did not implement Best in Class processes.

Level I Manual

After having implemented many different manuals, we believe the best were the ones written for Old Bakery and Asia Semi. The process maps developed for these organizations, to a large degree, show processes that align to the organizational work flow and not something written for conformance purposes. It is worth repeating the outlines here (Figure 13.1).

Here are some insights derived from studying the five process maps. Old Bakery, Asia Semi, and Aerco show the best process maps (process identification and interaction). The Middle East site has the weakest process map, since it mimics the standard to a large degree. Note the level of integration in each of the process maps (more than 95% integration).

Processes/Procedures

The processes and procedures are created by process owners working with cross-functional teams. The processes for the most part are developed in two-day workshops and then finalized by the process owners. Except for the Middle East site, most of the processes were developed in this fashion. For the Middle East site, most processes were developed by consultants and specialists due to the nature of the implementation. These case studies provide several good examples for process documentation. The Omnex process methodology uses document process flow charts as shown in Figure 13.2. Omnex also accommodates procedure style documents upon customer request, often putting the flow chart in the front.

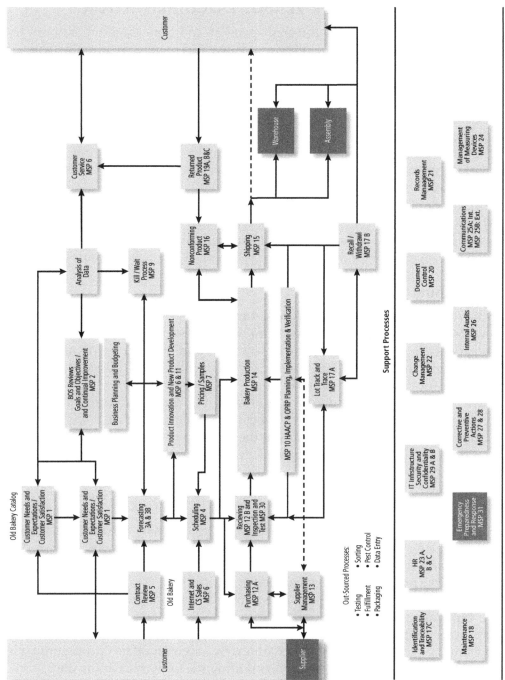

Figure 13.1 Old Bakery process map.

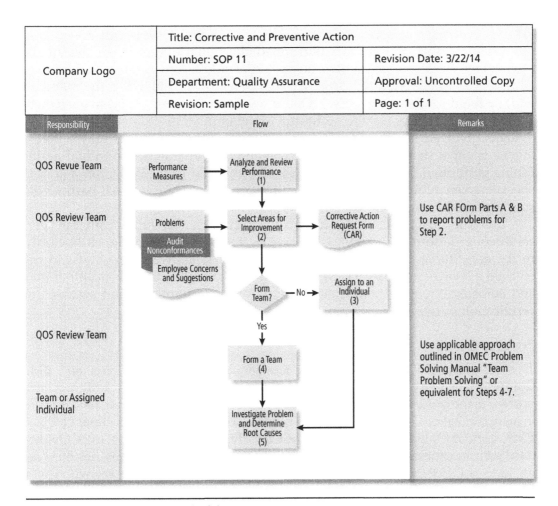

Figure 13.2 Omnex process methodology.

Good documentation follows a couple rules: Less is more (a flow chart should not be more than 12 steps long or three pages long). A process should include process control and specific performance requirements. (Forget the adage that if you include details in a process you are asking for trouble, and that you will get nonconformances from the auditor.) The authors recommend that you write exactly what and how you want a process to perform, ensure processes have process owners, and ensure that processes are measured, monitored, and improved.

Remember that processes are not functionally oriented; they cut across functions and/or sites. Some enterprise processes cut across sites and some site processes cut across functions. Automotive and aerospace companies identify customer oriented processes (COP) that have inputs from a customer with an output going to a customer. COPs are a way to identify customer-facing and other important processes.

Audits

For the most part, the authors performed the initial audits in all five of the organizations showcased in this book. Initial audits are always conformance audits (that is, determining whether the company is following the standard and/or the documented process). One drawback of an integrated management system is that it is not easy to audit due to the number of different management systems involved. If organizations are finding it difficult to audit an integrated management system, each system can be audited separately. Individual audits can be performed until the auditors learn or an audit team with QMS and EHS specialists can audit together. Another alternative is to have external parties who specialize in IMS audit the system.

After the management system becomes mature, the audit team can start conducting performance audits to ensure systems are performing satisfactorily. In the case studies discussed in this book, the systems were new and had not reached a level of maturity. However, some of the standards, such as automotive and aerospace, require performance audits of newly implemented systems for certification purposes.

Process Owners

This section could be titled "Process Owners, Process Measurables, and BMS Control Plans." Each of the implementations covered in the book assigned each process in the process map to a process owner. There is a natural owner for a process in an organization. Identifying process owners and giving responsibilities of QMS, EMS, and OHSMS is one of the biggest benefits of implementing IMS. Quality has been repeating the mantra "Quality is everyone's job." This is not the case for EMS or OHSMS. Creating process owners for integrated processes with QMS, EMS, and OHSMS responsibilities truly creates and distributes responsibilities companywide. This is the start of a culture change.

The BMS control plan shown in Figure 13.3 clearly identifies the process measurables and the target for each process. Each process owner understands that the process should be measured and improved, and this is the second part of culture change. Lastly, quality is understood to be for everyone in a company. To a large degree, environmental, health/safety, and food safety are confined to specialists. Implementing process owners and enterprise processes will bring about dramatic changes in an organization.

Business Management System Control Plan

Organization: _____   Product Description: _____
General Manager: _____   Issue/Rev Date: _____

Process Activity	Customer Req/ Expectation	Key Process/ COP	Measurement	Responsibility	Acceptance Criteria 2014 Q1, Q2, Q3, Q4	Review Frequency	Control Methods	Comments/ Reaction
				EXAMPLES				
Business Fulfillment	On-time delivery	K	% on-time in operations	Logistics	94, 95, 96, 96%	4/yr	Monthly management meeting	Corrective action after 3 consecutive
			% on-time to customer	Production control	100%	4/yr	Trend chart	C/A is more than 15% off target
Customer Complaint	Provide timely response	C	Complaint response	Quality	10 days	4/Yr	Production control dept	Continue to monitor
Design & Development	Meet timing requirement		Time to market	Design/dev	52 weeks	Weekly	Quality department	R, Y, G reaction
Business Creation	Innovation		Patents filed	Design	20 per year	Monthly	Design meeting	Continue to monitor

Figure 13.3 Business management system control plan.

Risk Management

Integrated risk allows an organization to understand the highest risk sites and events globally. As we discussed in earlier chapters, risk mitigation activities and testing to ensure controls are in place and working will help reduce costs for an organization in managing QMS, EMS, OHSMS, and social responsibility risks. For example, risk management and senior management's role and exposure to risk management and mitigation will become important topics in the next few years, especially with the advent of the new ISO 9001 in 2015 with risk identification and mitigation.

Registration

In all five case studies, the authors were able to help the organizations achieve registration to the respective standards. Achieving registration is almost like following a formula of steps, from initial assessment to roll out to internal audit to registration. This is a final step of a journey that in many cases should be the start of another one for organizational improvement.

SUMMARY OF THE FIVE IMPLEMENTATIONS

In this summary, we will highlight the pros and cons of each implementation.

Old Bakery had the most top management implementation support and also showed the most improvements. Cons were the mindset toward improvement and zero defects in the organization. It is a complacency and organizational malaise. This factor in conjunction with problem solving not getting ingrained in the organization will hamper this organization in the coming years.

Auto Tier One, the second case study that was cited, had top management support for the implementation. However, this organization did not see the improvements possible since they tried to integrate too much in a short six-month implementation. Some of the failures in implementation included the structure of the IMS manual, which appeared to be clause based. Also, the manual included the list of all documents including levels III and IV.

The Middle East site is the third case study cited in the book. This implementation followed the dictates of bid requirements that were fairly fixed from start to finish. The success in this implementation was the complete integration and certification of this process. One negative was the lack of top management involvement and the absence of process owner and employee interaction when the documentation was developed. However, the implementation was farsighted in implementing an integrated management system and evaluating risk as the construction was progressing.

The next two implementations cited in the book were Aerco and Asia Semi. In both organizations the goal was certification and there was little to no interest from top management in the actual implementation. The good news is that both organizations achieved certification. However, no real improvement ensued from the implementation other than the integrated management itself (and that is not a simple accomplishment). Both of these organizations are high tech and their focus is product development. Sometimes, high tech organizations do not always appreciate the value of business processes and management systems.

14

Integrating QMS, EMS, OHSMS, and FSMS

This chapter aligns QMS, EMS, OHSMS, and FSMS standards. Often times when implementers or auditors think about integration they are trying to understand how the clauses in the various standards align with each other. With the new high level structure (HLS) there is a natural alignment between the standards.

When we discuss integration, we will need to start with the idea of the process approach. Why? When we integrate, it has to be around processes. Each organization is made up of processes and this is defined in the process approach requirements of QMS (4.1). The processes of the organization must satisfy ISO 9001, ISO 14001, ISO 45001, and FSSC 22000.

To keep the focus of integrating around processes, let us reintroduce the enterprise and site processes we identified in Chapter 6, "How an Integrated and Standardized Management System performs for Maximum Effectiveness."

Enterprise Processes

- Policy, Objectives, Business Plan and Reviews (Performance Management)
- Sales and Contract Review
- New Product Introduction
- Scheduling to Delivery
- Training, Competency, and Benefits
- Direct Purchasing
- Customer Satisfaction
- Continual Improvement Programs (Performance Management)
- Internal Audits

Site Processes

- Manufacturing
- Receiving
- Shipping
- Corrective Action
- Preventive Action
- Risk and Change Management
- Calibration and MSA
- Nonconforming Product
- Indirect purchasing
- Document and Records Control

This chapter will focus on these processes for integration. Of course, actual processes and their sequence and interaction will vary from organization to organization. The alignment and arrangement of the clauses (see Table 14.1) were strictly around identifying which requirements of a particular standard a process should meet. Also, some clauses are not satisfied by processes. These clauses were purposely excluded.

Twenty-one enterprise and site processes essentially satisfy 95% of QMS, EMS, and OHSMS, and clauses. This is why integration is quite possible and feasible. Each of these processes can be implemented using a Best in Class method. Also, many of these processes can be implemented using an enterprise-wide integrated management system.

In many ways, the time for integrated management systems has arrived. More and more quality professionals and top management understand the benefits and savings to be achieved from an IMS implementation. We hope this book helps in this regard.

Table 14.1 Alignment and interaction of clauses.

Common High Level Structure (ISO 9001, 14001 and 45001)	Integrated Processes	Comment

4. Context of the Organization
  a. Understanding the Organization and its Context
  b. Needs and Expectations
  c. Scope
  d. Management System
	Context and Business Planning
	
	Additional Process Required
	Quality Manual
	Quality Manual (Process Map and Process Approach)
		This is a new requirement for ISO 9001, ISO 14001, and ISO 45001 standards from the revision of the standards from 2015 and 2016.
		Process maps and process approach is only present in ISO 9001 and is the basis of integration between QMS, EMS, and OHSMS.

5. Leadership
  a. Management Commitment
  b. Policy
  c. Roles, Responsibility and Authority
	Only Objective Evidence Required
	Quality Manual
	Organizational chart and job descriptions	

6. Planning
  a. Actions to Address Risks and Opportunities
  b. Objectives and Plans to Achieve Them
	Risk and Change Management
	
	Policy, Objectives, Business Plan and Reviews
		Implement integrated risk
		This requirement is new to ISO 9001.

7. Support
  – Resources
  – Competence
  – Awareness
  – Communication
  – Documented Information
	Training, Competency, and Benefits
	
	Document and Records Control	

8. Operation – Operational Planning and Control	Sales and Contract Review New Product Introduction Scheduling to Delivery Manufacturing Receiving Shipping Indirect purchasing Direct Purchasing Calibration and MSA	Includes control over all the processes in the organization (i.e., process map) and including manufacturing processes.

9. Performance Evaluation
  – Monitoring, Measurement, Analysis and Evaluation
  – Internal Audit
  – Management Review
	Customer Satisfaction
	
	Internal Audits
	Policy, Objectives, Business Plan and Reviews (repeat)	

10. Improvement
  – Nonconformity and Corrective Action
  – Continual Improvement
	Nonconforming Product
	Corrective Action
	Continual Improvement	

Appendix A
Integrating and Standardizing QMS, EMS, and OHSMS Management Systems– An Executive Management Primer

There is a proliferation of management system standards and requirements globally. These management system standards are either customer or industry mandated. Many standards are becoming a requirement for doing business (for example, ISO 9001, a quality management system standard with industry-specific versions such as ISO/TS 16949 for Automotive, ISO/TS 13485 for medical devices, and AS9100 for the aerospace industry; ISO 14001, an environmental management system standard; and ISO 45001, an occupational health and safety management system standard). There are yet other standards waiting in the wings that may soon become industry requirements for social responsibility or sustainability, laboratory management systems, and energy management systems. Typically, these standards are seen as hindrances or obstacles in the way of doing business and not beneficial.

Top management assigns these management standards to specialists in the company who then write manuals and procedures around quality, environmental, and health and safety management systems. The results are hundreds of procedures that impact the organization with multiple requirements for conducting a task (see Figure A.1). How can a business manage these standards most economically? Are there efficient methods for managing them?

Figure A.1 "I don't do quality, environmental, or health and safety, I just do my job."

The key to handling these standards efficiently is to understand the tremendous amount of commonality in requirements and expectations between them. For example, all of the management system standards require a policy, an objective, and a management review. Furthermore, each of them requires risk assessment and controls instituted for the risks identified. All of the standards require document and records control, internal audits, and corrective and preventive actions. This recognition of the common requirements has led to a methodology of integrated management systems (IMS) where requirements grouped together in the standard (called clauses) can be satisfied by a single business process. Businesses can economically and efficiently meet these standards with integrated and standardized processes that meet the requirements of QMS, EMS, OHSMS, and social responsibility. The goal of the primer is to make executive management knowledgeable of IMS and the steps that they can take in guiding their organization towards IMS. The appendix to this primer shows that most of the requirements of QMS, EMS, and OHSMS can be satisfied by approximately 40 to 50 processes in an organization.

Integration of Management Systems

All management systems evolve from the continual improvement cycle called Plan-Do-Check-Act (PDCA). This basic architecture has spawned common requirements in each of the steps of the PDCA cycle for the multiple standards. For example, in the planning step all management system standards include defining a policy, setting objectives, and creating a plan to meet the objectives and to evaluate the risks to the business. These common requirements of management systems can be met by common procedures or processes. This is a fundamental truth in the path to integrated management system standards.

Business Building Blocks are Processes

The fundamental organizational building blocks are the processes of an organization. This understanding is fundamental to integrated and standardized management systems. Businesses accomplish all tasks through processes that cut across functions of the business. See Figure A.2. All management system standards have requirements that are fundamentally fulfilled when processes perform a task. Processes are typically first documented and then taught to the employees of an organization. Figure A.3 illustrates a management system documentation pyramid.

The manual provides direction and guidance on how an organization meets quality, environmental, and/or health and safety requirements. The procedures explain how functions work together to accomplish the fundamentals of the business including sales, design, and manufacturing. Work instructions are at the task level and tell someone exactly how to conduct an operation in a process or procedure. Forms and checklists are filled out when employees perform tasks in a process.

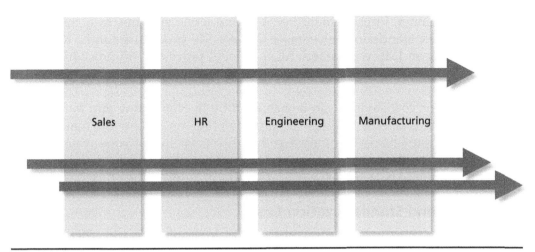

Figure A.2 Processes cut across the functions of the organization.

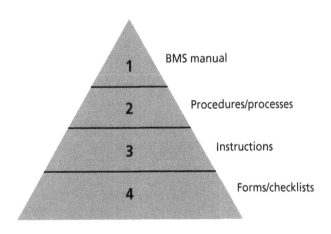

Figure A.3 Management system documentation pyramid.

Integrated Management System Standards versus Stand-Alone Management Systems

Organizations that implement management systems with specialists do so with stand-alone systems rather than integrated management systems (see Figure A.4). In most cases there is one documentation pyramid for each standard being implemented. In fact, if there are 60 procedures on average in each management systems of QMS, EMS, and OHSMS, then there are 180 procedures impacting the organization with 180 different process owners in stand-alone systems. In an integrated management system there are common procedures, what we call integrated procedures. In this example, sixty integrated procedures with 60 process owners is a definite improvement versus stand-alone systems. In a corporation with three sites, stand-alone systems will have 540 procedures and 540 process owners versus an IMS with standardized global processes, 60 procedures, with 60 global process owners. Less confusion and more efficiency is the hallmark of an IMS.

Tremendous cost savings can be achieved by implementing and maintaining an IMS. There is a cost savings in implementing an integrated management system in one site (that is, bringing together three systems into one system, called integration, and rolling out this one process to all the sites, called standardization). There are savings to both integration and standardization of the processes globally.

Integration and Standardization Costs

Integrated management system savings are 50% for implementation (of the second management system), 66% for maintenance, and 20% for third-party audits.

Integration and standardization result in 75% savings for implementation (for all sites after the first site), and 85% for maintenance. Reduction in third-party costs for multiple sites can be 20% of the third-party audit costs.

Savings from Integration for One Site

Assumptions: Cost of implementation of three management system standards, $200,000; maintenance costs, $90,000/year; and third-party auditing costs, $45,000 for three years.

Savings from implementation (one-time cost): $200,000 x .50 = $100,000.

Savings from maintenance: $90,000 x .66 = $60,000 per year at each site; NPV at 10% would be $600,000.

Maintenance includes maintaining stand-alone processes of QMS, EMS, and OHSMS, which will be combined to 1/3 of the previous total with 1/3 less process owners. Management reviews and internal audits will be 1.3 lower as well. Hence, maintenance of the QMS, EMS, and OHSMS will be reduced to 33% of the previous costs each year.

Savings from third-party audit costs: $3000 each year; NPV is $30,000.

20% of the third-party audit costs: the reduction is provided by registrars for integrated audits. Up to 40% is allowed for organizations with more than 10 sites.

Total Savings: $100,000 + $600,000 + $30,000 = $730,000.

*Company has no management system standards. Savings will not be the same if there are some costs for existing systems.

These savings are only for one site.

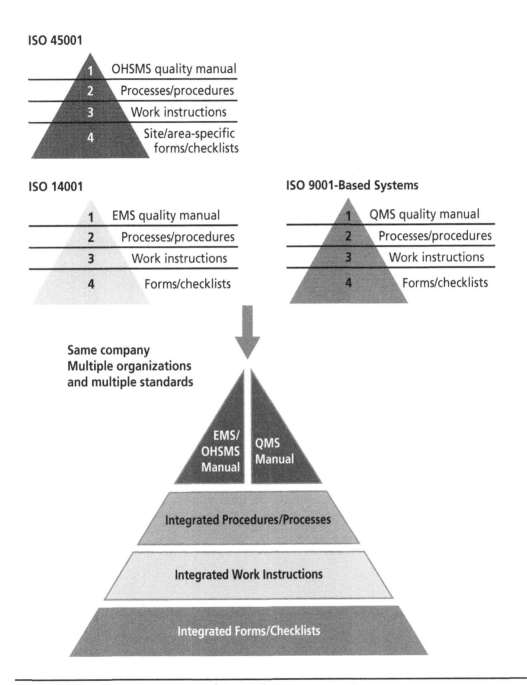

Figure A.4 Stand-alone systems versus integrated management systems.

Calculating Savings for An Enterprise

Using the same numbers as found in Chapter 1, let us assume that the per-site cost for implementing three management systems is $200,000, the cost to maintain all three non-integrated systems is $90,000, and third-party auditing cost for a three-year period is $45,000.

Savings in implementation costs for each site after the first one: $200,000 x .75 = $150,000 for each of the two remaining sites, or $300,000 for both of the sites.

Note: The savings for the first site is the savings from integration (that is, $200,000 x .50 = $100,000).

Total savings in implementation is $400,000.

Savings in maintenance costs per year: $90,000 costs for each site x .85 = $76,500 for one site or $229,500 per year for all three sites. NPV at 10% interest is $2,295,000 for all three sites.

Savings in third-party audit costs for three years: $45,000 x .20 = $9,000 for one site for three years or $27,000 for all three sites for three years. Savings in one year for all three sites is $9,000. NPV at 10% Interest is $90,000 for three sites.

There is an additional savings from doing integrated risk or using one methodology and reusing risk scores between sites. If we assume each site spends $50,000 each year to calculate risk for new products and processes, then the cost is $150,000 for the three sites and the NPV for integrated risk at 10% interest is $1.5 million.

Grand total for all three sites for integration and standardization is $400,000 from implementation plus $2,295,000 for maintenance plus $90,000 for third-party auditing, or $2,785,000 for three sites. When we include the integrated risk, savings increase to $4.285 million.

Is Our Organization's Management System Integrated?

From the previous section, we learn that there is a tremendous opportunity for savings from implementing an IMS in an enterprise. This is the reason that top management should be interested in implementing it in their organization. These hard savings are only the tip of the iceberg, with additional savings arising from the efficiency of the integrated processes. One of the first steps is to understand how integrated the organization's current management systems are. Here are some simple questions that top management can ask.

Key Questions

a. Have any of our sites integrated QMS, EMS, OHSMS, and other management systems?

If the answer is no, then proceed to the next set of questions:

- Does the organization have one manual?
- What percent of the processes and/or procedures of the management systems are common?
- What percent of the work instructions of the organization are integrated?
- What percent of the forms and checklists of the organization are integrated?
- Are there process measures for the integrated processes?
- Are there process owners for the integrated processes?

Proceed in this fashion to understand how many sites have integrated management systems.

b. Next, find out whether the sites with integrated processes have integrated the risk analysis for the QMS, EMS, or OHSMS.

c. Find out whether the integrated sites have integrated the audits.

This is the first step of IMS in an organization (that is, discovering the level of integration in the sites). Integration by itself saves money. Next we study standardization between the processes in the sites with integrated management systems.

d. Find out whether the sites that have integrated have also standardized their processes:

- Does the organization have one manual for the entire corporation or the sites that have integrated?
- What percent of the processes and/or procedures of the organization are common (or the sites that have integrated)?
- What percent of the work instructions of the organization are common (or the sites that have integrated)?
- What percent of the forms and checklists of the organization are common (or the sites that have integrated)?
- Are there global process measures for the global processes?
- Are there global process owners for the global processes?

In the book on integrated management systems we have numerically assessed the above.

When top management have asked the questions in this section, they should know which sites are integrated and to what percent. They should also know which of the sites have standardized and to what percent. See Table A1.1 for a site–process integration example.

Table A.1 Site–process integration example.

Site	Integrated	Manual	Procedures	Work Inst	Forms and Checklists
1	QMS – No				
1	EMS/OHSMS – Yes	100%	70%	0%	30%
2	QMS, EMS, OHSMS – No				
3	QMS, EMS, OHSMS – No				
4	QMS, EMS, OHSMS – No				

One site has integrated the EMS and OHSMS manuals and procedures.

Site	Standardized	Manual	Procedures	Work Inst	Forms and Checklists
1, 2, 3, 4	No				

There are no common manuals, procedures, work instructions or forms/checklists company wide. The answer is no, they have not standardized.

Making Sense of the Assessment

Conducting the assessment will be an eye opener for top management. It is the rare organization that has sites with integrated systems. However, if there are integrated sites, try to estimate to what percent the processes and the risk are integrated in each of the sites. In our example, there is much savings to be had in integration and standardization in the four sites. Of the four sites, only one has integrated EMS and OHSMS; overall, there is at most a 13% integration. There is 0% standardization between the four sites.

The savings numbers can be calculated using the numbers from our previous example ($5.2 million for the four sites). This is a combination of implementation, maintenance, auditing, and integrated risk savings.

There are many intangible savings—company-wide ownership of quality, environmental, and health and safety and knowing that the whole company is working with the same common processes.

How Do We Get Started?

Organizations typically start when top management is convinced about the need for integrated and standardized management systems. If this primer is not enough, start with an executive overview. If need be, the executive overview can be conducted after an initial assessment of the organization to figure out the percentage of current integration and standardization and the potential savings.

After the initial assessment an implementation plan can be drawn up to integrate and standardize the organization. As mentioned in earlier chapters, it is best to standardize about ten to 15 processes in a nine-month time frame and then continue the standardization process and do the next 10 or 15 processes later. Yes, all processes can be standardized in one go, but it is not possible to implement best in class processes while standardizing forty to sixty processes at the same time.

Companies can go forward with the confidence that standardization and integration works; the authors have been implementing them since 2002. The book includes five case studies of companies in the United States, Asia, and the Middle East in industries ranging from automotive, aerospace, and semiconductor to food and service.

Appendix B
Implementing Corporate Sustainability and Responsibility (CSR)

There are hundreds of CSR standards prevalent today. Most large corporations have implemented sustainability standards for themselves and their supply bases. Organizations are in many states of evolution in their CSR programs. Wayne Visser, the author of CSR 2.0 and a coauthor of "Creating Integrated Value" (below) says companies are somewhere in a continuum moving from defensive, charitable, promotional, and strategic to transformative.

Wayne, working with Chad Kymal, has identified a process that incorporates integration of quality, environmental, health/safety, sustainability, social and other standards that CIV calls $S^2QE^3LCH^2$ issues:

- S^2: Safety & social issues
- Q: Quality issues
- E^3: Environmental, economic and ethical issues
- L: Labor issues
- C: Carbon or climate issues
- H^2: Health and human rights issues

The CIV standard includes identifying stakeholder expectations (that is, interested party expectations), risk management, and management system standards integration, all topics of this book. The CIV methodology goes beyond integrated management systems to include business transformation and value addition. Hope you enjoy this bonus material on the integration of CSR into the management system.

Creating Integrated Value: Beyond CSR and CSV to CIV

By Wayne Visser[1] and Chad Kymal[2]

[1] Senior Associate, University of Cambridge Institute for Sustainability Leadership; Chair of Sustainable Business, Gordon Institute of Business Science; Founder, CSR International; Director, Kaleidoscope Futures; Vice President of Sustainability Services, Omnex. Website: www.waynevisser.com, Email: wayne@waynevisser.com.

[2] Founder and Chief Technology Officer, Omnex; Founder and President, Omnex Systems; Founder, American Quality Standards Registrar (AQSR). Website: www.omnex.com, Email: ckymal@omnex.com.

Abstract

Creating integrated value, or CIV, is an important evolution of the corporate responsibility and sustainability movement. It combines many of the ideas and practices already in circulation—such as corporate social responsibility (CSR), sustainability, and creating shared value (CSV)—but signals some important shifts, especially by focusing on integration and value creation. More than a new concept, CIV is a methodology for turning the proliferation of societal aspirations and stakeholder expectations—including numerous global guidelines, codes and standards covering the social, ethical, and environmental responsibilities of business—into a credible corporate response, without undermining the viability of the business. Practically, CIV helps a company to integrate its response to stakeholder expectations (using materiality analysis) through its management systems (using best governance practices) and value chain linkages (using life cycle thinking). This integration is applied across critical processes in the business, such as governance and strategic planning, product/ service development and delivery, and supply and customer chain management. Ultimately, CIV aims to be a tool for innovation and transformation, which will be essential if business is to become part of the solution to our global challenges, rather than part of the problem.

Article reference

Visser, W. and Kymal, C. (2014) Creating Integrated Value: Beyond CSR and CIV to CIV, *Kaleidoscope Futures Paper Series*, No. 3. Part of the *Kaleidoscope Futures Paper Series*.

Creating integrated value (CIV) is a concept and practice that has emerged from a long tradition of thinking on the role of business in society. It has its roots in what many today call corporate (social) responsibility or CSR, corporate citizenship, business ethics, and corporate sustainability. These ideas also have a long history, but can be seen to have evolved primarily along two strands—let's call them streams of consciousness: the responsibility stream and the sustainability stream.

Two Streams Flowing into One

The *responsibility* stream had its origins in the mid-to-late 1800s, with industrialists such as John D. Rockefeller and Dale Carnegie setting a precedent for community philanthropy, while others such as John Cadbury and John H. Patterson seeded the employee welfare movement. Fast forward a hundred years or so, and we see the first social responsibility codes start to emerge, such as the Sullivan Principles in 1977, and the subsequent steady march of standardization, giving us SA 8000 (1997), ISO 26000 (2010), and many others.

The *sustainability* stream also started early, with air pollution regulation in the United Kingdom and land conservation in the United States in the 1870s. Fast forward by a century and we get the first Earth Day, Greenpeace, and the UN Stockholm Conference on Environment and Development. By the 1980s and 1990s, we have the Brundtland definition of 'sustainable development' (1987), the Valdez Principles (1989, later called the CERES Principles), and the Rio Earth Summit (1992), tracking through to standards such as ISO 14001 (1996).

Weaving Together a Plait

As these two movements of responsibility and sustainability gathered momentum, it became possible to see their interconnectedness. Labor rights connected with human rights, quality connected with health and safety, community connected with supply chain, environment connected with productivity, and so on. The coining of the 'triple bottom line' concept of economic, social, and environmental performance by John Elkington in 1994, and the introduction of the ten principles of the UN Global Compact in 1999, reflected this trend.

We also saw integration start to happen at a more practical level. The ISO 9001 quality standard became the design template for ISO 14001 on environmental management and ISO 45001 on occupational health and safety. The Global Reporting Initiative and the Dow Jones Sustainability Index adopted the triple bottom line lens. Fair Trade certification incorporated economic, social, and environmental concerns, and even social responsibility evolved into a more holistic concept, now encapsulated in the seven core subjects[1] of ISO 26000.

Thinking Outside the Box

At every stage in this process, there have been those who have challenged our understanding of the scope and ambition of corporate responsibility and sustainability. Ed Freeman introduced us to stakeholder theory in 1984, John Elkington to the 'triple bottom line' in 1994, Rosabeth Moss Kanter to 'social innovation' in 1999, Jed Emerson to 'blended value' in 2000, C.K. Prahalad and Stuart Hart to 'bottom of the pyramid' (BOP) inclusive markets in 2004, and Michael Porter and Mark Kramer to 'creating shared value' (CSV) in 2011.

Typically, these new conceptions build on what went before, but call for greater integration and an expansion of the potential of business to make positive impacts. For example, Hart's 'sustainable value' framework (2011) incorporates pollution prevention, product stewardship, base of the pyramid (BOP) inclusive markets, and clean tech. Emerson's 'blended value,' much like Elkington's 'triple bottom line,' looks for an overlap between profit and social and environmental targets, while Porter and Kramer's CSV focuses on synergies between economic and social goals.

The 'How To' of Integration

Creating integrated value (CIV) takes inspiration from all of the thought pioneers who have gone before and tries to take the next step. CIV is not so much a new idea—as the longstanding trend towards integration and the ubiquitous call for embedding of standards testifies—but rather an attempt to work out the 'how to' of integration. When companies are faced with a proliferation of standards (Standards Map alone profiles more than 150 sustainability standards) and the multiplication of stakeholder expectations, how can they sensibly respond?

We have analyzed some of the most important global guidelines, codes, and standards covering the social, ethical, and environmental responsibilities of business—such as the UN Global Compact, OECD Guidelines for Multinational Enterprises, ISO 26000, GRI Sustainability Reporting Guidelines (G4), IIRC Integrated Reporting Guidelines, SA 8000, UN Business & Human Rights Framework, and Dow Jones Sustainability Index.

What we see are large areas of overlap in these guidelines, codes, and standards across what we might call the $S^2QE^3LCH^2$ issues, namely:

- S^2: Safety and social issues
- Q: Quality issues
- E^3: Environmental, economic and ethical issues
- L: Labor issues
- C: Carbon or climate issues
- H^2: Health and human rights issues

Our experience of working with business shows that most companies respond piecemeal to this diversity and complexity of $S^2QE^3LCH^2$ issues (let's call them SQELCH for short). A few large corporations use a management systems approach to embed the requirements of whatever codes and standards they have signed up to. Even, so they tend to do this in silos—one set of people and systems for quality, another for health and safety, another for environment, and still others for employees, supply chain management and community issues.

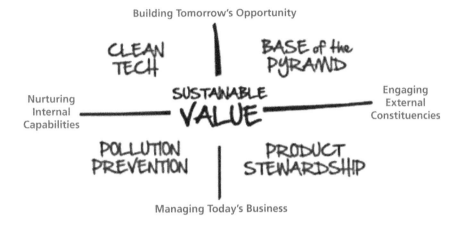

Figure B.1 Sustainable value framework.
Source: Hart, Stuart L. (2011). Sustainable Value.
Retrieved from http://www.stuartlhart.com/sustainablevalue.html

Knocking Down the Silos

CIV, therefore, is about knocking down the silos and finding ways to integrate across the business. In short, CIV helps a company to integrate its response to stakeholder expectations (using materiality analysis) through its management systems (using best governance practices) and value chain linkages (using life cycle thinking[2]). This integration is applied across critical processes in the business, such as governance and strategic planning, product/service development and delivery, and supply and customer chain management.

And what about *value*? Most crucially, CIV builds in an innovation step, so that redesigning products and processes to deliver solutions to the biggest social and environmental challenges we face can create new value. CIV also brings multiple business benefits, from reducing risks, costs, liabilities and audit fatigue to improving reputation, revenues, employee motivation, customer satisfaction, and stakeholder relations.

Pursuing Transformational Goals

Our experience with implementing and integrating existing standards such as ISO 9001 and ISO 14001 convinces us that, in order for CIV to work, leaders need to step up and create transformational goals. Without ambition 'baked in' to CIV adoption, the resulting incremental improvements will be no match for the scale and urgency of the global social and environmental crises we face, such as climate change and growing inequality.

One of the most exciting transformational agendas right now is the Net Zero/Net Positive movement[3], which extends the 'zero' mind-set of total quality management to other economic, social, and environmental performance areas. For example, we see companies targeting zero waste, water, and carbon; zero defects, accidents, and missed customer commitments; and zero corruption, labor infringements, and human rights violations. These kinds of zero stretch goals define what it means to be world class today.

Stepping Up To Change

In practice, CIV implementation is a six-step process, which can be described as: 1) Listen Up! (stakeholder materiality), 2) Look Out! (integrated risk), 3) Dig Down! (critical processes), 4) Aim High! (innovation and value); 5) Line Up! (systems alignment); and 6) Think Again! (audit and review). Each step is captured in Figure B.2 and briefly explained below. Of course, the process must also remain flexible enough to be adapted to each company context and to different industry sectors.

Step 1: Listen Up! *(Stakeholder Materiality)*

The first step of the CIV process is stakeholder materiality analysis, which systematically identifies and prioritizes all stakeholders—including customers, employees, shareholders, suppliers, regulators, communities, and others—before mapping their needs and expectations and analyzing their materiality to the business. This includes aligning with the strategic objectives of the organization and then driving through to result measurables, key processes, and process measurables.

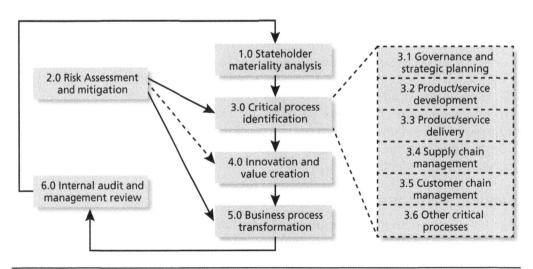

Figure B.2 Creating integrated value.
©2014 Wayne Visser and Chad Kymal

The stakeholder materiality analysis is the first level of integration and should be conducted simultaneously for quality, cost, products, environment, health and safety, and social responsibility. The analysis helps to shape a comprehensive set of goals and objectives, as well as the overall scorecard of the organization. When conducted holistically as a part of the organization's annual setting of goals, objectives, and budgets, it seamlessly integrates into how the business operates. A similar approach was developed and fine-tuned by Omnex for Ford Motor Company in a process called the Quality Operating System.

Step 2: Look Out! *(Integrated Risk)*

In parallel with the stakeholder materiality analysis, the risks to the business are analyzed through an integrated risk assessment. This means the identification and quantification of quality, cost, product, environment, health and safety, and social responsibility risks in terms of their potential affect on the company's strategic, production, administrative, and value chain processes. The risk measures developed must be valid for all the different types of risks and different entities of the business, and mitigation measures identified.

The first two steps of stakeholder analysis and risk assessment are requirements of the new ISO 9001, ISO 14001, and ISO 45001 (formerly OHSAS 18001) standards slated to come out in the next few years. For example, in the new ISO 9001 that is planned for release in 2015, it is called 'Understanding the Needs and Expectations of Interested Parties' and 'Actions to Address Risks and Opportunities.' The evolution of the ISO standards is indicative of a shift in global mind-set (since ISO represents more than 100 countries) to prioritizing stakeholder engagement and risk management.

Step 3: Dig Deep! *(Critical Processes)*

In step 3, the stakeholder materiality analysis and integrated risk assessment are used to identify critical business processes, using the process map of the organization. It is likely that the most critical processes—in terms of their impact on SQELCH issues—will include governance and strategic planning, product or service development, product or service delivery, supply chain management, and customer chain management. There may also be others, depending on the particular business or industry sector. This critical processes list should also include the most relevant sub-processes.

Step 4: Aim High! *(Innovation and Value)*

Step 4 entails the innovation and value identification element. Using the Net Zero/Net Positive strategic goals, or others such as Stuart Hart's sustainable value framework, each of the critical processes is analyzed for opportunities to innovate. Opportunity analysis is followed by idea generation and screening and the creation of a breakthrough list. This is the chance for problem solving teams, Six Sigma teams, Lean teams, and Design for Six Sigma teams and others to use improvement tools to take the company toward its chosen transformational goals. The improvement projects will continue for a few months until they are implemented and put into daily practice.

Step 5: Line Up! (Systems Alignment)

In Step 5, the requirements of the various SQELCH standards most relevant for the organization, together with the transformational strategic goals, are integrated into the management system of the organization, including the business processes, work instructions, and forms/checklists. Process owners working with cross-functional teams ensure that the organizational processes are capable of meeting the requirements defined by the various standards and strategic goals. This is followed by training to ensure that the new and updated processes are understood, implemented, and being followed.

Step 6: Think Again! (Audit & Review)

Integration has one final step, internal audit and management review, which creates the feedback and continuous improvement loop that is essential for any successful management system. This means integrating the value creation process into the governance systems of organization, including strategic planning and budgeting, management or business review, internal audits, and corrective actions. This is what will ensure that implementation is happening and that the company stays on track to achieve its transformational goals.

Words Count, Actions Matter

To conclude, we believe creating integrated value, or CIV, is an important evolution of the corporate responsibility and sustainability movement. It combines many of the ideas and practices already in circulation, but signals some important shifts, especially by using the language of integration and value creation. These are concepts that business understands and can even get excited about (whereas CSR and sustainability tend to be put into peripheral boxes, both in people's heads and in companies themselves).

More critical than the new label or the new language is that CIV is most concerned with implementation. It is a methodology for turning the proliferation of societal aspirations and stakeholder expectations into a credible corporate response, without undermining the viability of the business. On the contrary, CIV aims to be a tool for innovation and transformation, which will be essential if business is to become part of the solution to our global challenges, rather than part of the problem.

END NOTES

[1] Organizational governance, human rights, labor practices, environment, fair operating practices, consumer issues, and community involvement and development.

[2] It is interesting to note that the revised ISO 14001 being planned for release in 2015 includes a life cycle perspective for all aspects of operations including product design and delivery.

[3] This is captured eloquently in John Elkington's book, *Zeronauts* (2012).

Glossary

5S: Japanese methodology relating to the organization of the workplace to increase efficiency and reduce waste

AIAG: Automotive Industry Action Group

APQP: Advanced Product Quality Planning, a process used in new product development to ensure customer satisfaction (part of the Core Tools)

BMS: Business management system— Omnex refers to the QMS or the Integrated Management System as a BMS since it represents the entire business.

BOS: Business operating system— Omnex helped Ford Motor Company develop and train a methodology called QOS in the 1990s.

CCPs: Critical control points, used in food safety management systems to denote points in the food manufacturing process where failures could occur that might result in harm to the end user

control plan: Control plans, used to outline the system for measuring and controlling the levels of variation within a process

core tools: An AIAG mandated set of quality assurance tools for the automotive industry including APQP, PPAP, FMEA, MSA, and SPC

detection: Rating, on a scale of 1-10, the likelihood of detecting a certain failure mode (used in the FMEA process)

ERP: Enterprise resource planning software, used to manage every facet of a business from HR and payroll to new product development to ensure effective management

FAI: First article inspection, used to compare a sample item from a production run against the given specifications or requirements for that product

FMEA: Failure Mode and Effects Analysis, a system for risk assessment used throughout the entire manufacturing process to ensure that any potential failures of the product or process are addressed before they can affect the end user (part of the Core Tools)

GFSI: Global Food Safety Initiative

HACCP: Hazard analysis and critical control points, a system for risk management used in the food industry

KPIs: Key performance indicators, measures of an organization's performance against previously set goals or targets

LDAP: Lightweight Directory Access Protocol, a standard for accessing information within an organization's intranet or internet storage system

MSA: Measurement Systems Analysis, a process to ensure that measuring equipment is properly calibrated and the operators using the equipment will produce repeatable and reproducible measurements for the same item (part of the Core Tools)

occurrence: Rating, on a scale of 1-10, the probability that a certain failure will occur (used in the FMEA process)

Pareto charts: Bar charts used to show the most frequent occurrences of certain events or measures

PAS 99: British Standards Institution standard outlining the integration of management systems

Paynter chart: Tool used by Ford Motor Company to show actions taken over time

PPAP: Production Part Approval Process, a system for ensuring that a supplier can produce a product to the specifications and requirements of the customer (part of the Core Tools)

PPE: Personal protective equipment, used in the workplace to address safety concerns

PPM: Parts per million, a measure of the number of defects detected in a manufacturing process

QEHS: Combination of Quality, Environmental, and Health and Safety

QOS: Quality Operating System, implemented by Ford Motor Company

RFP: Request for proposal

RPN: Risk priority number, used in the FMEA process to organize the potential failures by priority and calculated by multiplying occurrence, severity, and detection ratings

severity: Rating, on a scale of 1-10, the severity of the effects to an end user if a certain potential failure were actually to occur (used in FMEA process)

"shalls/shoulds": In management standards, "shalls" denote compulsory compliance with whatever is outlined; "shoulds" are merely a recommendation of best practices or approaches and are not mandatory to achieve certification

Six Sigma: Methodology aimed at reducing variation within an organization

SPC: Statistical Process Control, a system used to track and reduce variation within a stable manufacturing process

SQF: Safe quality food

takt time: Calculation of the maximum production time per unit required to meet the demands of the customer

Bibliography

Kymal, Chad. What Works and What Doesn't in QS-9000 Implementation. *Automotive Excellence* (ASQ), Fall 1997.

Kymal, Chad. Juggling Multiple Standards: Save Time and Money by Integrating Your Various Management Systems. *Quality Digest*, June 2005.

Kymal, Chad and Gregory Gruska. *Integrated Risk Management for QEHS.* NIOSH Environmental and Health and Safety Symposium. South Africa, August 2009.

Kymal, Chad. *Integrating ISO 9001 and 14001*. ASQ Midwest Conference, Columbus, OH, March 2011.

Kymal, Chad. *Risk Management.* ASQ Midwest Conference, Columbus, OH, March 2011.

Kymal, Chad. *Integrating Social Responsibility (ISO 26000) with QMS and EMS, Pathways to Social Responsibility*. ASQ Pathways to Social Responsibility Conference, San Francisco, June 2011.

Index

Page numbers in *italics* refer to figures or tables.